INSPIRED

THE BREATH OF GOD

DOUBLEDAY

NEW YORK   LONDON   TORONTO   SYDNEY   AUCKLAND

INSPIRED

THE BREATH OF GOD

JOANNA LAUFER *and*

KENNETH S. LEWIS

PUBLISHED BY DOUBLEDAY

a division of Bantam Doubleday Dell Publishing Group, Inc.

1540 Broadway, New York, New York 10036

DOUBLEDAY and the portrayal of an anchor with a dolphin are
trademarks of Doubleday, a division of Bantam Doubleday Dell
Publishing Group, Inc.

Book design by Deborah Kerner
Title page and part title illustrations by Richard Waxberg

Library of Congress Cataloging-in-Publication Data

Laufer, Joanna.
Inspired: the breath of God / Joanna Laufer and
Kenneth S. Lewis.—1st ed.
p.   cm.
Includes bibliographical references and index.
1. Religious biography.
2. Inspiration—Religious aspects.
I. Lewis, Kenneth S.   II. Title.
BL72.L35   1998
291.4′092′2—dc21
[B]   98-15496
CIP

ISBN 0-385-48982-X
Printed in the United States of America
October 1998
First Edition
1   3   5   7   9   10   8   6   4   2

TO OUR DAUGHTER

S.D.G.

ACKNOWLEDGMENTS

We wish to thank the following people for their support, guidance, and generosity with respect to this book: Mark Chimsky, Elaine Markson, Mark Fretz, K. L. Hart, Kathleen Patterson, Reverend George Smith, Terry and Peter Hess, Chuck Hammer/Audio of the Americas, and John Kosner. We are also extremely grateful to the contributors.

Tobias Wolff

Leontyne Price

Herbert Benson, M.D.

Desmond Tutu

Kathleen Norris

Steve Reich

Ang Lee

Dr. Lorraine Hale

Pandurang Shastri Athavale

Rick Moody

Diana Eck

Kari Lee Hart

Mark Doty

Faith Ringgold

Madeleine L'Engle

Michael E. DeBakey, M.D.

Paulo Coelho

Christopher Parkening

Andre Dubus

Helen Baylor

Alexander Schindler

Thomas Moore

Howard Finster

Jack Polak

Dr. Rama Coomaraswamy

Wynton Marsalis

Simon Jacobson

Katherine Paterson

Vishwa Mohan Bhatt

Jean-Pierre Ruiz

Hakeem Olajuwon

Monica Chusid

Mark Richard

Dr. Lori Wiener

Alan Dershowitz

J. Carter Brown

David Checketts

Benjamin Hirsch

Walter Levine

John Polkinghorne

Gary Carter

Jeffrey B. Satinover, M.D.

Doc Watson

CONTENTS

Contents

AUTHORS' NOTE

All Scripture quotations, unless otherwise indicated, are taken from the King James Version. In the tradition of this translation of the Bible, we refer to the major sections of the Bible as the Old and New Testaments.

Throughout the book we use the masculine pronoun for God. In no way is this intended to suggest that God has only male attributes, or is exclusively masculine in nature. Rather, in keeping with tradition, the masculine pronoun He, or His, simplifies the language.

Forty-three people were interviewed for this book. Excerpts from their interviews are separated from our narrative by space breaks. After the design element (▣) appears, our narrative continues. Many of the contributors are quoted in several chapters.

PROLOGUE

When Benjamin Hirsch was six years old, he experienced such a hideous event that he blocked it out. He had to piece together the story from what he had been told by his relatives. The event happened on Kristallnacht. A group of Nazis came to his parents' house in Frankfurt, Germany, and demanded to see Hirsch's father. Hirsch's mother came to the door, holding one of her babies. She told the men, "Dr. Hirsch is not in, but I would be happy to have him call you as soon as he gets back." One of the men grabbed the baby from its mother's arms and threw it onto the floor. He pulled out his pistol, and pointed it at the baby. "You have thirty seconds to produce Dr. Hirsch," the man said. "If he doesn't come out, I'll shoot the baby first, then all the other children by age. One by one, you will see all of your children die." Hirsch's father had been hiding and listening in the back of the house. He ran out to his children, and was arrested. That was the last time Hirsch saw his father.

After his father was arrested in 1938, Hirsch's mother sent him, and his two older brothers and two sisters on a kindertransport to Paris. There the children were split up. His siblings were paired according to gender and stayed with different relatives, while he stayed with people who were not relatives. Hirsch then lived in several children's homes throughout France until 1941, when he came to the United States via an escape route through Spain and Portugal. Both of Hirsch's parents eventually died in concentration camps, as well as a younger brother and sister.

Despite all that he has been through, Hirsch has a strong faith in God. During our interview, he said he was inspired by God to keep going. In his work, he also feels God's direction, and a sense of his Jewish identity. Hirsch is an architect who designs and builds synagogues and churches. Among other projects, he designed the Holocaust Gallery, which is located in the William Breman Jewish Heritage Museum, in Atlanta—an exhibit that uses video, artifacts, and testimonies of survivors. When people walk through the exhibit—the dark lighting tight spaces—they see physical objects that make them feel as if they are actually entering a concentration camp. "In the ghetto section," said Hirsch, "I have an eleven-foot wall, which is the same height as the ghetto wall in Warsaw that was used to imprison Jews. I have a hole with a photograph of a child crawling out and bringing food into the ghetto. There are barbed wire fences with transparent pictures of people that are made of tempered glass, so that everybody who views this looks at the tempered glass and gets a reflection of themselves. You see yourself behind the barbed wire."

Very often in his work, particularly when he designs synagogues, Hirsch looks in the Torah for inspiration, yet he does not take credit for his inspiration or his gifts. "Whatever I'm able to do," Hirsch said, "I do by the grace of God." Hirsch had the following to say about his experience as a survivor, and about his faith.

BENJAMIN HIRSCH

My situation is a little bit unique in that I'm a child survivor. I am not a child of survivors, but a child survivor, which is different from the adult survivors. Children learn to adapt to the world as they fear it, and I adapted to life in Germany. Hitler came into power four months after I was born, and I adapted to that for the first six years of my life. That was what was there for me. I adapted to whatever situation there was for me in France. What I have had the hardest time dealing with is not the role God played in what happened to my family, but the fact that I was a teenager before I realized what really went on. I think about seeing my mother for the last time at the train station as she said good-bye, watching her pack for me before we left, watching her tears drop in the suitcase, and not knowing why she was crying or what she was feeling. I have had trouble dealing with the fact that I was not in touch with what was happening to me and to my extended family, but I do not blame God. God gives man free will, and lets us fend for ourselves. Sometimes He intervenes. I am not so strong that I could get through something like this on my own. The intervention, the inspiration to keep going, came from God.

I don't understand many things that happen. I am troubled by many events, but I feel God's presence in the good and in the bad. My understanding of God is that He is not limited by what we, as human beings, are limited by. Our limits of knowledge, our physical limits, our intellectual limits, are not comparable to God's omnipotence. There is a wonderful story about the Bal Shem Tov, the great rabbi who is considered to be the founder of the Hasidic movement. The Bal Shem Tov was standing high on a hill with a couple of his students, looking down at the town where his school was. Suddenly, a group of Cossacks on horseback attacked the town. As he saw many of his students, along with the men, women, and children of the town being slaughtered, the Bal Shem Tov looked up to heaven and said, "Oh, if only I were God." One of his students said, with astonishment, "But, Master, if you were God, what would you do differently?" The reply was "If I were God I would do nothing differently. If I were God, I would understand."

Hirsch's story is not a story about inspiration in the way that we ordinarily think about inspiration. We tend to think about biblical inspiration, or about inspiration in relation to our work and creativity, but not in relation to our pain. Yet, when we go through hardships and trials—though we often credit our healing to emotional support, resilience, and time—many of us, like Hirsch, sense a mysterious stirring within us. It is a stirring that tells us that something larger than us is at work, that something is filling our spirits and inspiring us to press on.

We will never be able to understand a gun pointed at an infant's head, the loss and cruelty experienced during the Holocaust, but, like Hirsch, we may be able to understand—in hindsight, or as it happens—that God is present in our blessings and in our trials. We read in the book of Job that "there is a spirit in man: and the inspiration of the Almighty giveth them understanding" (32:8). To know this is to know our limits as human beings. We do not, on our own, have God's understanding. We do not have His vision. When we become inspired, we are granted a moment of hearing or seeing what we ordinarily do not hear or see. We are filled with an elevated understanding and vision that lifts us up above our grief, that empowers us, and that elevates the quality of our work.

This book is about inspiration, specifically divine inspiration, based on the stories of people who have experienced it in their lives. In different ways they have been inspired by God in their work, or in the midst of hardships. The word *inspiration* has been so overused, and in such a generic way, that it could convey just about anything at all. But in the stories that follow, we will see it at work. When the divine Spirit enlivens people, there is the hope that, in turn, this will stir the spirits of others. The aim of this book is to show how the Spirit of God has inspired people of our time in their lives, love, work, and trials, people who have influenced our lives.

Our lives, of course, include Ken's life and mine. We requested interviews from the contributors to this book because, over the years, we have admired their books, their music, their art; and we have followed the work they have done with (and for) others. Beyond being moved by their work, we have felt the *life* in it. Their stories exemplify that inspiration is the source of that life.

Through colleagues and research, we were also introduced to contributors after the book was already under way, such as Holocaust survivors Hirsch and Polak, as well as Levine, who is in remission from a very rare type of cancer, and Chusid, who suffered the loss of a child. As it turned out, a number of the other contributors who are known for their work spoke about inspiration not only in relation to their profession, but also in terms of overcoming hardships. In their trials and suffering, they believe that God gave them vision and peace, and that the Spirit of God revived them.

Inspiration is a term often used when speaking about God's influence on the biblical writers. People of faith believe that these writers were inspired by the breath of God, that their words, in Scripture, are God's words. This work of the Spirit is not the same as the inspiration behind works of art, music, or literature, or of any other field where the human spirit is involved. But just as similar things are not completely the same, they also are not completely different. We must recognize that just as an artist's spirit is involved in works of art, the authors of the Bible had creative input, as well. They had different degrees of passion, different vision, and different writing styles. If God's Word passed through their minds and souls, what came out was expressed in their unique styles and, therefore, colored by them.

At times, biblical inspiration conveys an image of God dictating words to various individuals, and the words being transcribed by those individuals, with different degrees of understanding. Occasionally, it happens to almost every writer (though by no means *only* to writers) that what they are creating seems to come to them effortlessly, and to come from beyond them, as if they, too, were transcribing the words of someone else. Thinking of this scenario, we might picture a diligent but detached person mechanically typing away. The image might suggest that the person's creative role in this process is passive and inert. Yet this is hardly the case.

Flannery O'Connor spoke to this issue when she wrote that

Even if one were filled with the Holy Ghost, the Holy Ghost would work through the given talent. You see this in Biblical inspiration, so why think that it would be different in a lesser kind of inspiration? If the Holy Ghost dictated a novel, I doubt very much that all would be flow. I doubt that the writer would be relieved of his capacity for taking pains (which is all that technique is in the end); I doubt that he would lose the habit of art. I think it would only be perfected. The greater the love, the greater the pains he would take.[1]

The contributors to this book are hardworking and passionate. Those of them who associate their creativity with God do not claim that God creates *for* them; at times, *through* them, but not *for* them. They still put into action the gifts that He gave them. It is because they are in motion that they are able to be moved. God's breath would serve no purpose to these people if they were not engaged, the way wind would serve no purpose to an anchored sailboat. In all that they do, their passion and faith drive them to do it more fully. If greater love is what gets them to take greater pains, in that love is inspiration.

Though inspiration often comes when one is in motion, it is common for those who are inspired to feel the sense of doing nothing, of being vessels that are filled with revelations. The composer Antonín Dvořák had been known to view his extraordinary work as a composer as being inspired by God. He spoke of his talents as "God's voice," claiming, "I simply do what God tells me to do."[2]

How do people know that the voice they are hearing is God's

voice? What makes them believe that this voice is not their own? Talking about inspiration is the same as talking about God. It is impossible to prove the existence of either. But in the stories of people who claim to be inspired by God, a common theme is that what they accomplish is of a quality beyond what they feel they can take credit for, and they accomplish it with ease. Another is that they have a revelation that completely changes the course of their work and their lives. One could certainly argue that this inspiration could be coming from instinct, passion, or a muse, but the people who claim to hear God are often the people who seek to hear God. They make themselves available to listen to Him in prayer. In some cases, they consider their music, their poems, to be their prayers.

The author Madeleine L'Engle claims that daily prayer is as essential to her life as her daily work. She has said,

> *To work on a book is for me very much the same thing as to pray. Both involve discipline. If the artist works only when he feels like it, he's not apt to build up much of a body of work. Inspiration far more often comes during the work than before it, because the largest part of the job of an artist is to listen to the work, and to go where it tells him to go. Ultimately, when you are writing, you stop thinking and write what you hear. To pray is to listen also, to move through my own chattering to God, to that place where I can be silent and listen to what God may have to say.[3]*

To accept that prayer is not a monologue, that God not only listens but responds, is a matter of faith. But to believe this means that we believe that God responds, not with a big booming voice, but to the heart—the way the heart speaks to us about love. And when we make ourselves available and do hear (or feel) this response, it is subtle but unmistakable, like the act of breathing.

Prayer, of course, is a choice. For us to pray, to give thanks, or to voice our questions and doubts shows that we are choosing to leave an opening in our spirits. Without this opening, there is no vessel, no place into which God can breathe.

In the Bible, when God created Adam, He "breathed into his nostrils the breath of life; and man became a living soul" (Genesis 2:7). In the creation of Adam's spirit we see that breath in humankind began with the breath of God.

The Hebrew word *ruach* means "breath," "wind," and "spirit." "The spirit of God hath made me, and the breath of the Almighty hath given me life" (Job 33:4). Just as the word for *spirit* in Hebrew is the same word for *breath,* the word *breath* is often used in place of the word *inspiration* in the Bible, and vice versa. The following verse from Job 32:8, which we looked at earlier (p. 16), as well as several translations of the same verse in Scripture, reads: "But there is a spirit in man: and the inspiration of the Almighty giveth them understanding." In other translations of the same verse, the word *breath* appears instead: "But it is the spirit in a man, the breath of the Almighty, that gives him understanding" (NIV).

The fact that there are different translations of Scripture shows that the hands of human beings are involved. Skeptics have often dismissed the whole notion of divine inspiration, claiming that people created the story of God in the Bible—that it is man's creation of God, not God's creation through man. There are those who point to different verses in Scripture that they believe to be inconsistent and inauthentic. The subject of the order of the canon (the order in which the books of the Bible appear) is also discussed. For one thing, the order of the canon in the Hebrew Bible is different than it is in the Christian Old Testament. Both Jews and Christians edited and revised these sacred writings, and their choices influenced how the books of the Bible were arranged.

We note here the different sequences of books in Jewish and Christian Bibles, and any questions regarding their contents, in light of divine inspiration, for this book is about inspiration. It is not a work of theology or scholarship, nor does it set out either to contradict or to reinforce the positions of critics or fundamentalists. What we have to ask is, How do human beings, who are willful and who make choices, respond to inspiration? If four people met Jesus tomorrow, and He said the same thing to each one of them, would they necessarily write about it the exact same way, even if God guided them? Whether they are vessels for God or not, they are still human, and their different visions and limitations would influence the way they would respond to being prompted by God. And yet, in the four different versions of what these individuals would write would be the essence of what Jesus had said. Likewise, the fact that the order of the books of the Bible is not the same does not mean that the essence of the Bible—its overall message—has changed.

Divine inspiration is different from what people speak of when they say that a painting or a book or a person has inspired them. We are often moved by paintings, books, and people—they can make a difference in our lives—but art, literature, and human beings are not, by themselves, divine. Though the painter, the writer, the people we meet may have been divinely inspired by God, neither they nor their work are the *source* of inspiration. They are the *products* of what God has inspired. And yet, God will use people and their work to show us the divine. When we receive the work, we will feel the life in it. What God has breathed in, the work will breathe out.

Inspiration, as well as faith, often transcends the intellect. It is felt and reflected in the lives of people who believe that God has inspired them. This book provides story after story about how well-known (and lesser-known) people have claimed to have been inspired by God in their lives, love, work, and creativity. Many say that it was God's presence that brought them to peace in the midst of extreme challenges—the death of a child, a parent, a sibling, a lover, living with cancer, AIDS, mental collapse, becoming crippled as the result of a charitable act.

We want to learn what inspires creative and influential people, because what they produce in the world enriches our lives. Since the individuals we interviewed believe God inspires them, we are able to learn how their spiritual beliefs and practices enhance their lives and creations. The majority of these individuals are not theological masters; they are masters in their respective fields who have all felt directed, in different ways, by God. In some cases, this is the first time they have publicly shared their spiritual views.

Readers can find knowledge and wisdom from reading the stories of people whose work has moved them already on an artistic and professional level, but whose spiritual beliefs they may not have known. For those of us, like Ken and me, who live with faith but not without doubts, it is encouraging to see how faith relates to everyday life. We all want peace in the midst of challenges, inspiration that guides our lives and work, and a deeper sense of love. The people we interviewed sense that their talent and standards of excellence come from a spiritual source. We want to give readers who may admire the work of these contributors a chance to know, and learn from, this often private aspect of their lives.

The way people might affect others is always one of the thoughts behind their actions and work. Making ourselves available to inspiration, knowing that we may move or motivate others will only make our lives richer and more compelling. The common theme in every one of the stories you are about to read is that despite the widely varying backgrounds and professions of the contributors to this book, they have all been guided, encouraged, consoled, and healed by the Spirit of God.

THE BREATH OF GOD

I am a practicing Catholic, but I find myself hesitant to label myself that way. I have a feeling that God leads people to that place where they can find Him, and this is where I have been led. I think the real point is to be obedient to the powerful encouragement and inspiration that you feel, from time to time. I have learned to recognize and pay attention to the promptings I feel, because there is a history now of what happens when I do that, and when I ignore them. And in such ways you come to recognize the presence of God in your life.

TOBIAS WOLFF

"Music is serious theology," observes Kathleen Norris in *The Cloister Walk*. "Hildegard of Bingen took it so seriously as a gift God made to humanity that in one of her plays, while the soul and all the Virtues sing, the devil alone has a speaking part. The gift of song has been denied him."[1]

What do the soul and the Virtues have that the songless devil does not? After all, plenty of out-of-work souls and Virtues that were cast in a play would welcome a speaking part. But singing, the Psalms tell us, brings us joy and freedom, and can be an act of praise to God. Neither of which the devil has nor does. The Bible portrays him as having glee but not joy, freedom only to a point, and he refuses to give God praise. Because the singer is both performer and instrument, a living vessel for the song, the singer's spirit is both open and filled. "Be filled with the Spirit"—God's Spirit—the Bible says, "speaking to yourselves in psalms and hymns and spiritual songs, singing and making melody in your heart to the Lord" (Ephesians 5:18,19). The devil refuses God's Spirit and this is what separates him from God.

To receive God's Spirit is to be inspired, and inspiration is not about vices against virtues, or bad versus good. It is a gift, and it comes not by will but by grace to anyone who is open to receive it. Inspiration and the spirit are associated with the image of breath, the divine breath that gives us life and invigorates our lives. In Scripture we read that God breathes in us and through us, that His Spirit fills our spirits. "The spirit of God hath made me, and the breath of the Almighty hath given me life" (Job 33:4). To inspire literally means to breathe into. When we release our last breath, we *expire.* When we are *inspired,* we feel energized, creative—more fully alive.

Breath is at the heart of singing, for it is the singer's breath, voice, and spirit that produce the song. Those who chant or sing spiritual songs tell of entering into a deeper level of worship, understanding, freedom, and joy when they sing, which deepens their faith. Secular singers and performers have also felt inspired when they sing. And just as breath is not only inside us but comes out of us as well, the breath of God that inspires us can come forth and move others. We have all felt joy and freedom and spirit come bursting out of a singer's song. We respond not just to notes or melody, but to the passion in both, to the *life* that is in the music. It either enlivens us or it leaves us cold. It fills our spirits, or it does not.

In our conversation with Leontyne Price, the internationally re-nowned opera singer, she said that she believes she is in "communion with God" when she sings. Born in 1927 in Laurel, Mississippi, Price was the grandchild of Methodist ministers on both sides of her family, and her parents were very active in the religious community. Price's introduction to singing came in church. As she puts it, "Church was where it all started for me musically. Playing the piano for the adult choir and singing in church as a child formed a very strong background. I felt nurtured by the belief, at an early age, that when I sing, or express myself in any way as an artist, that this is as close to God as I can ever feel." Whether performing operatic arias, German *Lieder,* or American spirituals, the thread that has connected all of Price's performances is her steadfast belief that the inspiration she receives comes from the Spirit of God. "I still have this total feeling of being in direct contact with God, as if I am touching Him when I sing. It has given me the strength that I still have as a per-former."

This is one of the first times that Price has publicly discussed her art in relation to her faith. She believes that the breath of God is at work in the breath that produces the human voice.

LEONTYNE PRICE

Singing is a very personal art form. An instrumentalist has to deal with, and touch, another object—a violin, a piano, etc. However, singers are the object of the art, and singing is the most personal way to express art. It is you, and you are it. The breath that is involved with singing is a technical thing. It is part of the training that helps to produce the voice in the best form possible. But breath, in terms of the Spirit of God, is really about the sense I get of being in the hands of God when I sing. I really do feel that I am in touch with something much higher than myself, and much higher than the performance that I am giving. I am in the hands of God, who guides me far beyond any technical expertise that I may have.

I never go out on the stage without praying. I have to have that moment before I go on stage, because I will not go out without letting God know that I need His strength. One night I was supposed to perform, and I was very ill. This happened in Dallas. It was the opening of the wonderful new hall there, in 1989. My recital was supposed to be the first one held there. As always, I took time to pray before, and somehow I was able to get to the stage. I leaned on the piano because I was very weak and ill, and I prayed silently after each note, as if saying to God, "It's really not up to me alone. It's up to you and me." I will always remember that night because I probably did the best singing I have ever done. With every note, I felt God's presence. After the performance, I was taken to a hospital and diagnosed with diverticulitis.

I think that all artists are vessels, and that we are guided in the way that we express our art. I feel so grateful to God that He gave me the gift of being able to sing. I cannot believe that any artist does not acknowledge that his or her art was a gift from God. It has been said of the composer Giuseppe Verdi that he was an agnostic. I do not believe that you can compose the Verdi *Requiem* and be an agnostic. *Libera me, Domine* ("Deliver me, O Lord"). How can you include that without knowing to whom you are speaking? Who are you asking to free you? Who are you asking for salvation? There is only one God, and if you put yourself in the hands of God you *will* be free. Whenever I sang the *Requiem,* my own experiences and my total belief in the omnipotent merged so completely. Conductors have told me that it seemed as if I were having an out-of-body experience when I sang it—that I was someplace else, though, of course, always in the music, but outside of just the notes. In every performance that I have ever done of Verdi's *Requiem,* it felt as if God wrote every note.

To be perceived as being out of one's body, or to have the sense of being out of one's body, is to have the sense of being breath and spirit alone. Though we cannot literally be out of body as long as we are alive, there is the sense that we do get, on rare occasions, of being so involved and self-abandoned, so focused and detached at the same time, that we feel as if we are being lifted up above ourselves, watching ourselves doing what we are doing. This is one of the aspects of inspiration—not the feeling, necessarily, of being out of one's body, but the sense that our spirits are operating on a higher level of involvement and understanding, that we are being lifted up above ourselves.

Take any of our five senses out of our bodies and we could still survive. Take our breath out of our bodies and we could not. We have this in common with everyone who is alive; we all live on the air we breathe. The image that we generally have of God is that He is somewhere in the air, somewhere above us in heaven. But air is above us, around us, and inside our lungs. As the author Agnes Sanford has observed, "We live in God. That's what we breathe."[2]

In the Bible, God created Adam and caused his spirit to come to life by breathing into his nostrils. The image of God breathing is an image that appears not only in the Bible, but also in ancient myths. When writing about the respiratory system, Mary Kittredge tells us that

> *In an ancient Australian creation myth, a god brought two mud figures to life by breathing into their mouths, noses and navels. . . . In the ancient South Sea kingdom of Fiji, people with breathing ailments were thought to be losing their souls. . . . Also in Fiji, people were sacrificed on shore as the new boat of a chief was launched; the dying breaths of the victims were thought to provide 'good luck wind.' . . . And in early Rome, a dying person's next of kin had the right to inhale the sufferer's final breath and thus his spirit.*[3]

Breath is linked to the spirit even in the words we speak. The Hebrew word for spirit is *ruach,* and *ruach* can also mean breath or wind. In other languages as well, the word for spirit is also the word for breath. In Latin it is *spiritus,* in Sanskrit it is *pragna,* and *pneuma* is the word used in Greek.

The breath of God is not, in a literal sense, the air that fills the lungs. It is divine breath that fills and enlivens the spirit. In turn, the "voice of God" that people speak of is not usually a loud, thunderous voice from heaven. It is not a human sound that fills our ears, but something divine that fills the spirit and the heart. We know what is being said, not by actually hearing it, but by feeling and perceiving it the way we feel and perceive love.

In our conversation with Dr. Lori Wiener of the National Cancer Institute in Maryland, she talked about how children claim to hear the voice of God through divine messages of inspiration. Dr. Wiener, a social worker and coordinator of the Pediatric HIV Psychosocial Support Program, grew up with what she calls "a conservative Jewish background," and confesses that her faith in God did not develop or deepen until she began working with children who have AIDS. She also talked about how children living with AIDS have claimed to have received messages of comfort through visitations from children who have already died of the disease.

DR. LORI WIENER

Working with children who have AIDS and their parents often challenges one's basic faith—whether a child is going to die, or a parent is going to die before a child. The children, even the young children, talk about what they think dying and the afterlife are like. When one of them is actually taking his, or her, last breath, and I'm with them, I pray for a peaceful transition. My belief in God, and in the power of God, helps me to achieve peace in the midst of the whole dying process. However, my spiritual life did not lead me to do the work I am doing. It is my work that has given me a deeper spiritual side.

I think that the reason my work has deepened my faith in God is because the children I work with talk about their experiences so vividly and spiritually. There is one story that moved me tremendously. A little girl was sitting down at the table with her mom, eating soup, and all of a sudden she just looked up and stared into space. She moved her eyes like she was following something, then she picked up her hand and started waving. She said, " 'Bye, 'bye, Allen. 'Bye, 'bye." The girl's mother said to her, "Honey, what are you doing?" And the girl said, "I'm saying good-bye to Allen. He's with Jesus." So the mom said, "Allen is fine, honey. Allen is fine." Less than a half hour later, the phone rang to say that Allen had died.

So many children and parents report stories like this to me. A child might say, "Someone's come to visit me a few times." Then the child would see, in a photo album, a photograph of someone who had died and say, "That's the person who has been visiting." Or they say a

deceased brother or sister has come back, and they did things together.

One child, who was fourteen at the time, actually gave me the
name of a child who had died in that room a year before, and the
name of another child who had died a year and a half earlier, and he
told me that these two children had come to visit him the night
before. He said they had just walked straight through the window,
and he showed me the window. He said, "They just came straight
through and they told me that I shouldn't give up at this point, that
although people don't think I have any more time, I still do. It's not
my time yet." This child was very sick at the time, and I remember
asking him about what the experience was like for him. I asked him if
it was frightening. And it wasn't. He said it was very comforting. He
wanted the dead children's parents to know that the children are well,
what they looked like, and what they said they were doing.

I have asked the children, "Tell me how they talk to you." And
they have said, "I hear everything they say, but they never move their
lips." I always ask this question, and over the years I have yet to hear
someone tell me that the person who has come back to visit them has
ever moved their lips. I don't know what that means. For most of the
people, it has been very comforting. Frequently, when a person is very
close to death, and they tell me that people who have died are in the
room, my experience has been that usually, within hours, this person
is going to die, too.

Through my experiences with these children, I have developed a
very strong sense of God's presence, and a very strong belief that this
is one life, and there's a transition to another existence from here.
From the stories I consistently hear, it has all been very positive, and
there's no sense of time. The children tell me that they are told from
the kids who come back to visit that the transition is going to seem
really fast, that it won't feel like days, weeks, or months have gone by,
that there is no reason to worry.

I have lost and I have known so many people who have lived and who have died. I feel incredibly privileged to have known them, to have helped them through the journey of this world. There are some days that are very difficult. I'll be on the street, and I'll see someone who looks familiar, only to remember that no, this person has been gone a long time now. What keeps me going and gives me peace amid all that I've seen is my faith in God. I have heard the question—If there is a God, then why is there AIDS? Why not? you could say. Why me? someone could ask. Well, why not me? I have also been asked how I can constantly work with people who are dying. I'm not. I'm working with people who are living, and with God's inspiration I'm helping them to live. Even when you're dying, on your last breath, you're very much alive.

Those of us who have been present at someone's "death" bed know that though the person may appear lifeless, though we know that death may be seconds away, we do not fully accept his parting until the person breathes for the last time. What we are holding on to, of course, is not the person's respiration, but the spirit inside the breathing, living man.

This is why so many people choose to speak of loved ones as "living with" AIDS, as opposed to "dying of" AIDS, or of any other disease. A few weeks before a friend of mine who had AIDS died— though he had, for months, lost the use of his arms and his legs—he said to me, "I have been walking again, and it is so wonderful." I am not sure to this day if what he had at the end was the most merciful dementia or a vision, but he saw something that, for the moment, revived him.

Visions and visitations occur throughout the Bible, and come through the Spirit of God. It is the life-giving Spirit of God that reveals, enlightens, and inspires. In the Old Testament, the Spirit of God, the breath of God, descended upon the prophets and made God known "unto [them] in a vision" (Numbers 12:6). In the New Testament, it was also the Spirit of God that was "poured out" at Pentecost. When this happened, Peter, quoting the prophet Joel, said to the people who had gathered in Jerusalem, "Saith God, I will pour out of my Spirit upon all flesh: and your sons and daughters shall prophesy, and your young men shall see visions, and your old men shall dream dreams" (Acts 2:17).

Claiming to have had visions, visitations, or to have received a word from God is a claim that is either real or invented, a miracle or a delusion, but always the miracle is a mystery. To accept that God can get across to us a message of hope, of inspiration, involves faith. It involves an openness and a willingness to believe what can never be proven or fully explained. Whether God gives us revelations in the manner that he gave to the children that Dr. Wiener cares for, or whether he gives us revelations in subtle ways, there is a movement from the divine Spirit to the human spirit.

In the Bible, this movement of the Spirit began before there was a human spirit to move to. At the beginning of creation, the "Spirit of God moved upon the face of the waters" (Genesis 1:2), and made life and light out of darkness. When God created Adam, He breathed into Adam "the breath of life; and man became a living soul" (Genesis 2:7). And it was the Holy Spirit that Jesus breathed into the spirits of his disciples (John 20:22).

One of the gifts that the Spirit breathes into our spirits is healing. This does not mean that we are spared all sickness or death. What this means is that in the midst of sickness and death, God is there. He breathes new life into us. He expands our human, limited vision and lets us see beyond our sorrow and our fears.

It is often asked, If God is so powerful, why does He allow us to suffer? Why doesn't He take our suffering away? The questions *Why, God?* and *Why me?* that Dr. Wiener brought up are addressed more fully in the following chapter, but in this chapter we look at two stories that involve the healing and inspiring breath of God, which revived two people in pain, and gave them a desire to help others.

The first is that of the legendary folk and bluegrass musician Doc Watson. Blind almost from birth, he has had to live without seeing, which calls for faith. With great dignity, he talked to us about the death of his son, Merle. Over ten years ago, a few weeks before Merle died in a tractor accident, as if Watson had sensed it coming, he asked his son, "If death were to come, how is it between you and the Lord?" Merle replied, "Dad, I have made peace with God. I'm not afraid to die." In three weeks, Merle died, and from then on began the loss, the grief, and the divine inspiration that kept Watson going.

DOC WATSON

My son, Merle, was a dear boy, and I loved him. When he grew up, he wasn't only a good son, he was as close a friend as I'll ever have in this world. He was killed in a farm tractor accident. It flipped over on him and crushed his chest. He died almost instantly, and he didn't suffer. The flat part of the blade that pushes dirt on the front came down and caught Merle on the side of his head. He was unconscious instantly. It might have been a merciful death. It turned out that Merle had a brain tumor, and we didn't know this until after he was dead. We found the papers with the diagnosis in the specialist's files. They say that death from a brain tumor is a horrible way to go. So things happen as they will. And if we could change the future—if we knew it and could change it—we might make it worse. I am glad we are governed by God, and not by man.

I've never really gotten over Merle's death. When I think about it now, I miss him more than I did when it happened, but my faith in God has given me peace. The spirit of God guides every detail of my life. Even when I don't deserve it. I have had to deal with the loss of a child, and I have been given the strength and inspiration to overcome. This is not human strength alone. It is instigated by the Almighty, as is every blessing in my life.

I recorded a gospel album in 1990 called *On Praying Ground,* and I dedicated the album to the memory of Merle Watson. Folks usually call my music traditional, with bits of country, bluegrass, rockabilly, and even some jazz added in. But gospel music is very dear to my heart. In fact, my dad, General D. Watson, was the singing leader in the little country Baptist church in Deep Gap, North Carolina, where I grew up. In the liner notes of *On Praying Ground,* I added some Scripture to go along with each song. I added John 11:25,26 for a song called *I'll Live On.* In this Scripture, Jesus says, "I am the resurrection, and the life: he that believeth in me, though he were dead, yet shall he live: and whosoever liveth and believeth in me shall never die." One of the photos for the album was taken in an old-time church. I sat on a bench, and I said, "Lord, if the Gospel in this album will inspire one human soul, it will be worth all the effort. I don't care if I make any money on the record or not. I've done this out of love for the Gospel. It has inspired me and increased my faith, and it might inspire others." I don't know if faith has been easier for me than it is for a sighted person, but there's more to us than just our five senses. Even people who can see can't see the future. God can.

Remember the job you lost, or the man or woman who broke your heart, the one you are now grateful for because you were brought something better? How is it that a random conversation about death can take place three weeks before the death of a son, whose quick, painless death from a blow to the head would later reveal a tumor? We cannot see the future, and we sometimes have to look back to see the signs that something was working in our behalf.

But all is relative. We do not have the wide-angle, all-encompassing vision of God. Our losses hurt, our pain is real pain. We are not healed by being told that God's timing is best, that heaven is a better place, that our loved one has been spared suffering. We are healed by being breathed back to life with the love that only the breath of God can give.

Watson's sense that something beyond his strength and his vision had entered his spirit and healed him is similar to what was experienced by David Checketts. In 1995, Checketts was named president and chief executive officer of New York City's Madison Square Garden. He currently oversees all operations of the Garden and its two sports franchises—basketball's New York Knickerbockers and hockey's New York Rangers—as well as the MSG television network and Radio City Music Hall. Though he is the head of his company, and has an often grueling schedule, Checketts sets aside every Sunday that he is not working to teach a Bible study to adults at the Mormon church that he attends in Connecticut. Sometimes Checketts has to prepare for these studies in the back of a car as he travels to and from work, or on an airplane. He was also the bishop of the church that he previously attended in Salt Lake City, when he was the president and general manager of the Utah Jazz. The bishop's duties, he explained, involve "counseling people who are going through difficult times, conducting funerals, weddings, and blessings for babies. So when I wasn't in my office making trades and going to games, I was doing all of this."

On the night before we met with Checketts, Hilton Hotels Corporation had initiated a hostile takeover of ITT Corporation, the parent company of Madison Square Garden—an attempt which eventually failed. But in the midst of it, even with the phone calls and frantic knocks on his office door, Checketts neither canceled our interview nor allowed it to be interrupted. He spoke about a death in his family that he had once felt responsible for.

DAVID CHECKETTS

When I was twenty-seven years old, I became the president of an NBA team, the Utah Jazz. My wife and I had found a house in Utah to move into, and my older brother, Larry, who was thirty-one at the time, came over to help us move. Larry was an undercover narcotics cop and was consumed with getting people off drugs. He was constantly putting his life in danger, but he was committed to helping others. Well, we started moving furniture in a truck over to our new house. On one trip, we were going up the street and some of the furniture started to shift, so my brother said to stop for a minute. I stopped, and he got out. He got up on top of the truck, held down the furniture, and told me to drive slowly. So I started to go, and we still don't know why this happened, but Larry fell off the truck. I had driven a little bit before I realized he had fallen. When I saw that he wasn't there, I jumped out of the truck and looked back, and there was already a crowd gathering around him. I ran back as fast as I could, and I could hear him screaming. He had landed right on the back of his head, and he was bleeding from both of his ears, and he was screaming my name. I knelt there in the street and held him in my arms. He couldn't tell where he was or what was going on, but he was screaming my name, and screaming for God to help him and to release him from the pain. Suddenly, a helicopter was there, and it flew him to a hospital. I had to go over and get his wife and four young children, and then I had to go get my parents, and I took them to the hospital. In three days, Larry died.

C. S. Lewis said that finding God at a time that you experience death is like going up to a house with all the lights on, hearing that someone is inside, but no one will come to the door. That's what happened to me. Over the next three months I became despondent. I couldn't play with my kids because I felt guilty about Larry's kids not having a father. I couldn't take my wife out because I felt guilty that his wife was alone. And I would go to work and deal with athletes who were interested in money and not much else, and I would think I should become a police officer and carry out what my brother was doing. I sunk lower and lower until, as much as my wife has always loved me, I think she was ready to leave me.

One day my father came to my house. I sat with him sobbing, saying this was unfair, how could this happen, how could the God in heaven allow this to happen to me? My father said that I was feeling sorry for myself and not helping anyone. He added, "Why don't you just decide to live your life as a tribute to him?" It was at that moment that I realized the extent to which I *was* feeling sorry for myself, and not trusting God. I had closed myself off to His comfort, and to the faith I used to have. I generally feel the Spirit of God through prayer, but this time I felt it just come upon me. I suddenly felt a surge of love for Him, and from Him, and though the situation hadn't changed, this love was changing something in me. I no longer felt angry and hopeless. I believe in the gift of inspiration, and I believe that God cares very much for us, and that He uses His Spirit to guide people who need inspiration.

The Bible says that the rain falls on the just and the unjust. Everyone, at some point, suffers. But I find that there is a significant difference in how people who have faith and people who do not have faith deal with their suffering. At that time in my life, I needed help, I needed comfort, I needed wisdom, I needed courage, and without God, I couldn't get past my grief. I had lost my faith until God provided it. God inspired me to live my life as a tribute to my brother, and since that time I have made sure that our athletes go to schools and give anti-drug messages to students. My faith has shown me that there is a purpose for my being here that goes well beyond anything I do professionally. There are things that are so much more important than whether or not the Knicks beat Miami on Sunday, and there are things that are much more important than whether or not we made our budget last quarter. I rely on Him to help me keep this in focus.

To discover one's purpose in life in the midst of a hardship is to be faced with re-creating one's life. We ask, Who am I now without what I lost? Who am I to do this?

Though we may feel lost, we move forward, often cautiously at first. We do not always trust that there is something beyond our pain. And yet sometimes, in the midst of our pain, we become inspired to take action in our lives, even if we first wonder if we are up to the task. We may feel led to create with a new vision, or to fulfill a new purpose in life because we see things that we had not before seen— things we sometimes do not feel ready to see. When the angel of the Lord appeared to Moses in a burning bush and Moses was asked to bring the Israelites out of Egypt, Moses did not say to the Lord, I'm your man. He said what many of us who have felt called by God have said: "Who am I, that I should go . . . ?" (Exodus 3:11).

Who am I? We say it all the time. We hear something inside us telling us to take a step forward, and we think—You must mean someone else. We forget that God knows what He is calling us to do. He knows our humanness and our imperfections. The author Madeleine L'Engle addressed this subject during our conversation when she said, "It has always been an irony that God, the Holy Spirit, often uses people with rather dissolute and terrible lives to produce great works of art. I can't think of any great artist whose life was consistent with his art except for Bach. I like that God chooses and inspires unqualified people. If you were going to start a great nation with children as many as the stars, would you pick Sarah, a woman past menopause, and Abraham, a man who was a hundred years old? A friend of mine said, 'Hebrew Scripture is full of old men in long beards saying to God, "You want me to do *what?*" ' "

Inspiration and revelations come whether we are prepared or not, and will often point us in a new direction. We can see this kind of revelation at work in the creation of Hale House. Hale House was founded in 1969 by Dr. Lorraine Hale and her mother, Clara Hale. Located in Harlem, in New York City, Hale House is a nonprofit home for children who are born addicted to drugs, and whose mothers cannot care for them.

Dr. Lorraine Hale shared with us her belief that the idea for starting Hale House was inspired by God, and that this revelation redirected her life.

DR. LORRAINE HALE

Back in the late sixties I was a guidance counselor in the [New York City] public schools, but I felt I wasn't making a difference in the children's lives. My mother was a foster mother, and she kept saying that God had put me on earth for a reason, and that He would reveal that reason to me. One day, after I left her house, I was sitting in my car waiting for a stoplight to change, and I saw a woman on the sidewalk, sitting on a wooden crate, and nodding off. She was holding something on her lap, and I thought I saw it move. I didn't think it was a dog or cat. When the light changed, I drove about a block or so, then decided to take another look. When I did drive back, I sat in the car watching the woman for a while, and I saw that what was under her arm was a baby. I asked the woman if she was all right, and I could tell by looking at her—I knew the look—that she was on heroin. I quickly told her who my mother was, and I wrote my mother's name and address on a slip of paper and gave it to the woman. Though my mother had taken care of children for years and years, she had never before taken a child off the street, and when the woman showed up, my mother wasn't very pleased. She didn't want a drug addict in her house. Mother suggested that I get another job to help take care of this baby. And I did, working with her. That was how we got started. This child was the first drug-addicted baby we ever cared for.

I believe that God had given me the revelation that my mother said He would. I literally changed directions—my car and my life. If you can understand this, there was nothing that I did that *I* did.

I can't think of anything I have *ever* done that would have made Hale House work, other than our prayers. The staff prays and so do the children. The inspiration that I get for new programs comes as a result of our prayers. My sense of religion is that God is. Whatever we call God, God is. And to the extent that we allow it, He leads our lives. If you ask me if I've done anything remarkable, I don't think so. I've done things that people are supposed to do that are very human, and I have been very blessed. When I come to work, I'm greeted by the children. I do a little dance for them when I see them, and they appreciate my humor. I'm glad God revealed to me that I should be here, working with these children. Even in getting the funding to start Hale House, there was divine intervention. I had written a proposal to get funding, and I submitted it to an agency. When I found out we were going to be funded, I said, "That's great, that's really good," and I asked if I could have a copy of the proposal back. The proposal I received was nothing like the proposal I had written. My original proposal was probably the worst-written proposal in all the world. It was horrible, even grammatically. Someone had rewritten our proposal and submitted it. I don't know who that person was. I will never know. Have you ever heard of anyone doing such a thing without taking credit or money or something? That was God in action. I would like to think of Hale House as a house of God.

The sense of doing nothing, which Dr. Hale speaks of, of being a vessel, is a common feeling among those who are inspired. But ironically, we generally find that those who are most inspired are also the most productive. Dr. Hale, who holds doctorates in child development and developmental psychology, is one of those people. In addition to pioneering the treatment of drug-addicted mothers and caring for their babies since 1969, she and her mother (who passed away in 1992) have also founded a home for mothers and their babies who have AIDS, and have established various programs to aid and educate children and adults on the subject of drugs.

Though Dr. Hale may be productive and hard at work, her belief is that the Holy Spirit guided her so that, as she put it, "there was nothing that I did that *I* did." The Spirit filled her without her prompting. In the Christian faith, receiving the Holy Spirit is more about faith than anything else. At the heart of Christianity is the belief that those who accept Jesus Christ as Lord and Savior will receive the Holy Spirit. In the Bible, Christ promised his disciples, just before he was crucified, that "the Counselor, the Holy Spirit, whom the Father will send in my name, will teach you all things and will remind you of everything I have said to you (John 14:26—NIV). And as He was about to depart to heaven, He said to them, "You will receive power when the Holy Spirit comes on you; and you will be my witnesses in Jerusalem, and in all Judea and Samaria, and to the ends of the earth" (Acts 1:8—NIV). And when it did come, at Pentecost, this breath of God, it came with "a sound from heaven as of a rushing mighty wind" (Acts 2:2).

To Christians, God is Father, Son, and Holy Spirit. The Holy Spirit is the third person of this Holy Trinity—He is as much God as is God the Father and God the Son. They are not separate gods, but different manifestations of one God. Christians pray to the Father through the Son, with the guidance of the Holy Spirit, who not only guides and empowers but comforts, heals, counsels, reveals, and inspires.

When speaking with Katherine Paterson, author of children's literature, she said that "The Holy Ghost is the marriage between God the Father and God the Father-Creator. There is the God that we cannot know, and Jesus—the God that we can know, who the Holy Spirit gives us the possibility of knowing. It is one God that we know in different expressions. I think that a lot more people have an experience of God as Holy Spirit than they do of any experience of God."

The Jewish concept of the Holy Spirit, and of inspiration, is that though the Spirit of God is within—"All the while my breath is in me, and the spirit of God is in my nostrils" (Job 27:3)—revelations are the products of what one does. Importance is placed on saying daily prayers, performing rituals, and doing good deeds which are called *mitzvoth.* There is faith, but revelation and understanding are not believed to be the products of faith. Through the *doing* comes revelation and understanding.

We spoke with Rabbi Simon Jacobson, a member of the Lubavitcher movement of Orthodox Judaism. He is the author of *Toward a Meaningful Life: The Wisdom of the Rebbe,* in which he presents, for the first time in English, the teachings of the legendary Lubavitcher leader Rabbi Menachem Mendel Schneerson. In our conversation, Rabbi Jacobson talked about the Jewish concept of the Holy Spirit: "In Hebrew, *ruach* means 'spirit,' " Jacobson said, "and *kodesh* is 'holy.' *Ruach Hakodesh* means that the Holy Spirit of God is shining through a person's being, so they, in a sense, have an ability to see beyond what most of us, with our conscious minds, are able to comprehend. From a Jewish point of view, the concept of Holy Spirit means that people who have sublimated themselves through selfless service, dedication, and prayer has elevated themselves to a place where, rather than indulging in their own needs, they become a servant of God. They can then become a channel for divine revelation and manifestation. You consistently find in Jewish history people who had those qualifications and had that ability. It's linked, to a degree, to the person's faith, but it's much more connected to the person's effort in the performance of *mitzvoth* and, in general, to their dedication to God that permeates and affects their entire behavior."

Does it matter whether or not the breath of God inspires because of what one does or because one has faith? Either way, the Spirit is a gift from God, and it seems that it would matter more that we are open to receive it. Christians believe that they receive the Spirit through faith, yet they also perform religious rituals and good deeds. Jews focus on rituals and good deeds, yet they also have faith. Diana Eck, Professor of Comparative Religion and Indian Studies at Harvard University, is a practicing Christian who maintains that her faith has been strengthened by what she has learned from other faiths. She told us that "Breath is the inspiration and the expiration, you might say, of the divine. In Christianity, Judaism, and other traditions, there is the sense that the breath—or the spirit, the energy of God, associated with breath—is life-giving and creative. In the Hindu tradition, breath is the icon of the divine in ourselves. There is the term *prana,* or 'breath,' which is the image of the life within, and which connects us with a wider reality. It is a vehicle for the realization of *atman,* or 'the spirit within,' a word which also means 'breath.' In another vein, there is the language of Shakti, or the outpouring energy of God— that aspect of God that is intimately involved in and energetic in the world. Shakti conveys the sense of divine enlivening energy—like the creative spirit and breath in the biblical tradition."

During our conversation, Professor Eck suggested that we contact Pandurang Shastri Athavale, an Indian savant-philosopher, who lives in Bombay, India. Athavale (pronounced *Ah-TAH-vah-lee),* Eck explained, is a man who has literally launched a spiritual revolution in thousands of Indian villages. At the core of this revolution is the idea of relating self with God and God's creation. It is not only about having an understanding of the love of God, but also about the importance of how individual actions reflect that love. We contacted Athavale in India, and began a series of correspondences.

"Breathing," Athavale explained, "is the most critical function of human life. One is alive because one breathes. Yet, nobody knows how to breathe. What is known is that we inhale air and the oxygen contained in that air is used to purify blood. Once used, the impure residue is thrown out of the human body through exhaling. What is remarkable is that this most crucial function of our body, on which our existence depends, happens without our conscious efforts. We continue to breathe even when we sleep. Therefore, the Vedas [sacred books of ancient Indians] say that God is the life-giving breath. All other religions, too, say the same thing. People may call breathing a natural process, or a mechanical function, but I see God's active presence behind it. Every breath carries God's signature."

Athavale is the leader of a grassroots spiritual movement that the United Nations recently named as one of the most significant developments in the world. This movement, known as Swadhyaya (pronounced *swah-DEE-ah*—a Sanskrit word that roughly translates to mean 'self-study'), includes practitioners of various religious paths, whether they be Hindu, Christian, or Muslim, and has been quietly spreading across almost all of India. It is not a replacement for one's religious path, but rather a reinforcement of it.

"To me," Athavale said, "everyone is a child of the same God, and I thought that the true meaning of *bhakti* [devotion] should be conveyed to all people. They should be told that gratefulness is the basis of *bhakti,* and that *bhakti* is not complete without action."

In 1954, with around twenty coworkers, Athavale began visiting the villages around Bombay to spread a message of love for God and love for all people. He encouraged villagers to devote some portion of their work and talent to God by volunteering for community projects.

The tangible results of this "devotional" work were the development of small and large agricultural farms, the building of fishing and dredging boats, the cutting of diamonds, and so on. The produce and money obtained from these ventures has been used to meet the economic needs of society, and to aid the needy members of that society.

What started out modestly in 1954 has grown dramatically. As Athavale's vision of Swadhyaya has evolved, he has also been joined by a diverse group of professionals—doctors, engineers, lawyers, accountants, and teachers—who offer their talent, time, and energy out of love and gratitude to God. These professionals devote some time—perhaps a day every few weeks, or four days per month—as an offering to God in a community enterprise. For every one hundred participants, this translates to four hundred work days a month. To date, Swadhyaya has spread to nearly 100,000 villages across India and is estimated to have directly improved the lives of 20 million people.

In 1997, Athavale was awarded the Templeton Prize for Progress in Religion, which has been awarded annually since 1973 to a person who has advanced an understanding of God and/or spirituality in an extraordinary way. Valued at 750,000 pounds sterling, about 1.21 million dollars, the Templeton Prize is the world's largest annual monetary award. This is especially noteworthy in the case of Athavale, who has never sought or requested monetary donations.

PANDURANG SHASTRI ATHAVALE

Through Swadhyaya, people learn that human life cannot exist without the existence of God, and that the human body, the supreme creation of the world, is a gift of God. God does not live in a distant heaven, or in a temple. He lives in one's heart. This understanding becomes the turning point in one's life. One's life takes on a new purpose. Love of God becomes the inspiration and motivating force, and one becomes inspired to live and work for others in society in the same manner—without expecting anything in return.

In my work, I have tried to motivate people to work for God out of devotion to Him. God directs my life. A human being should express his gratefulness to God through devotion of time and talent for His work. Swadhyaya is a process, a way of life and of thinking that expanded in a geometric progression. What started as a very small trickle has been transformed into a perennial flow that has changed the lives of millions.

We Swadhyayees work selflessly in society as children of the same God, and try to establish selfless relations. We expect nothing. We leave aside monetary gain, position, and status—we do not even expect the appreciation of society. This kind of motivation can come only out of love for God. This idea of selfless love and selfless work has been derived only from God. He loves us, that is why we are alive. He works for us silently without expecting anything in return.

Through Swadhyaya, one comes to know that the one Supreme God is not different from the spark of the divine within, and that one is related to the other like a wave is related to the ocean. By being conscious of the underlying oneness of our source we call God, and our relationship with that source, we can face the limitations imposed by individual life situations. I experience His presence in every step of my life, and in each breath.

Breath is spirit, and God is spirit, and we have within us breath and spirit and God.

"It is not surprising," Professor Diana Eck said, "that a great many of the meditation traditions—Hindu, Buddhist, and Christian— really begin with the attention to the breath, simply because breath is the focus that we always have with us. Returning to the breath is, in a way, returning to our deepest and truest selves. There is no one kind of inspiration. Christians find inspiration in a variety of ways. Some by their commitments to justice, and to work in the world. Some by their devotional or Pentecostal experience of being filled with the Spirit of God. Some through liturgies and forms of ritual enactment that are inspirational. But the breath of God, the Holy Spirit, is not somehow tied to the steeple of the church. It is truly free. In the words of Saint John's Gospel, 'It blows where it wills' (3:8—RSV). It is active in the whole of creation, and in the religious lives of many people. The language of the Holy Spirit reminds those of us who are Christians that God touches, inspires, and is present in the lives of all people."

LOSS, GRIEF, AND HEALING

WHERE IS GOD?

So my crippling is a daily and living sculpture
of certain truths: we receive and we lose, and
we must try to achieve gratitude; and with that
gratitude to embrace with whole hearts
whatever of life that remains after the losses.
No one can do this alone, for being absolutely
alone finally means a life not only without
people or God or both to love, but without
love itself.[1]

ANDRE DUBUS,
Broken Vessels

"While making the bed and boiling water for coffee, I talk to God," says the character Luke Ripley in "A Father's Story," a short story written by Andre Dubus. "I offer Him my day, every act of my body and spirit, my thoughts and moods, as a prayer of thanksgiving. . . . This morning offertory is a habit from my boyhood in a Catholic school; or then it was a habit, but as I kept it and grew older it became a ritual. Then I say the Lord's Prayer, trying not to recite it, and one morning it occurred to me that a prayer, whether recited or said with concentration, is always an act of faith."[2]

Like his character Luke Ripley, Andre Dubus talks to God. "I pray for everything," he said during our interview. "I prayed for the Holy Spirit to be with us today." There are very few authors who, at the heart of their work, have the high stakes and moral challenges that are present in Dubus's. In "A Father's Story," a man of faith who, because of his religion, will not even allow himself to remarry chooses not to report a hit-and-run car accident that his daughter is responsible for, to protect her, knowing that the victim of the accident will die.

Like the men and women of faith he writes about, his own life is a testimony of challenges and faith. In 1986, Dubus was struck by a car and lost a leg. His accident was the result of his genuine love for people and his generosity. As he was driving home from Boston shortly after midnight, he got out of his car to assist two people in trouble. The car that hit Dubus (and eventually caused him to have his leg amputated at the knee, and to lose the use of his other leg) also fatally struck one of the people he was trying to help. In an effort to raise money for Dubus and his family, Ann Beattie, E. L. Doctorow, Gail Godwin, John Irving, Stephen King, Tim O'Brien, Jayne Ann Phillips, John Updike, Kurt Vonnegut, and Richard Yates held benefit readings at the Charles Hotel in Cambridge, Massachusetts.

Our interview with Dubus took place at his house in Haverhill, Massachusetts. There are ramps leading up the steep hill of his driveway. Many paintings by his children hang on the walls inside. Some were actually painted on the walls. As he shook my hand he said, "I'm tired and grumpy. How are you?" But he never seemed grumpy, and he never seemed tired. He was in and out of rooms receiving deliveries—mail, food, and items from the pharmacy—pulling books he referred to off of bookshelves to show us. His Bible, which he read a passage to us from, had many pages marked with papers and looked as if it had been through extensive use. Dubus said that prayer and his faith in God were instrumental in his healing, and that his gratitude to God has increased since his accident.

ANDRE DUBUS

The accident was in 1986. I was coming back from Boston, shortly after midnight. It was a clear summer night. How many lanes are there on Route 93? Well, I was in the middle one. Ahead of me was a car, broken down, no taillights, but it was a very clear night. I could see the car. I didn't even have to put on the brakes. There was a woman at the emergency call box, calling, so I thought—That's taken care of. I'll just go by the driver's side and see if there is anyone injured who may need first aid. So I went into the speed lane. And there was a woman standing beside a car, bleeding from the face and crying. The woman was hysterical and she said, "There's a motorcycle under my car." I looked at the road, and there was a black pool, and I thought it was blood, that there was a crushed guy under there. There was no traffic, so I thought, I have to get her off the road. I thought she was in danger of shock. And I thought, I have to go back and see if there's something alive, and that was what was horrifying. Then her brother, whom I had not seen, came out from around the trunk. He said, *"Por favor. No hablo Inglés.* Please help." Later, I learned that the woman had run over a motorcycle, which a drunk guy had fallen off of—a very, very nice drunk guy. He fell asleep going sixty miles an hour on a motorcycle. Fell off, walked away, and abandoned it. What I had thought was blood was just oil. Anyway, when I got the woman and her brother to the side, finally a car was coming. I was waving it down because I wanted another person with me to go look under there, at what I assumed was a motorcycle and a crushed person. The woman driving the car I waved down did not see us, and she did not see the disabled car, because it had no rear lights. She was in the speed lane. She saw my car's red blinking emergency lights, and turned right. That's when she saw the disabled car. Then she swerved back to the left, and that's when she took us out. Bad night for everybody. The guy got killed. The brother. He didn't get through that night.

Sometimes I tell my daughters, "You know, I almost took Route 125 that night, but I thought, no, 125 has dangerous curves, I'll stay on Route 93." But when I say that, it doesn't sound real. I'm grateful to God because I shouldn't be alive. The woman who hit me was going sixty-five when she put on the brakes. I still have my upper body. I came out with a brain, no paralysis, still alive for my kids. I'm grateful for every breath.

I never heard that word—*grateful*—much until I got crippled and met cripples. The first one I remember meeting was a one-legged lesbian biker. She was taken off. Crotch high. She said, "I left my leg as a hood ornament." I said, "Hell, I knew they were going to take my leg off because I was in the hospital for weeks. They were trying to save it. What was it like to wake up without one?" She said, "Interesting you asked that. I woke up on a gurney. I knew my leg was gone. I'm a graphic artist. I looked at my hands, and I was grateful." I think that was the first time in my life that I really heard that word. I don't plan on getting through a day without using it anymore.

I also never get through a day without praying. I pray for everything. Day and night. Every morning since I started writing in college, I've always prayed, "Please help me to write well of you and for you." I pray before I teach, go on a date, be with anybody. Some priest came to see me after I was crippled, and he said, "Just try to walk in the Lord." I thought, That's a good, tactful thing to tell a man on wheels. But I do what he said before I'm with other people. I just walk in the Lord. I say, "Holy Spirit, you just talk for me. God will give the answers." I have absolute faith in that.

See, never say things like, "Next year we'll go to Barcelona." I used to say, "I'm a slow writer. I gestate for a long time. I have enough notes in my notebook to last the rest of my life." And I did, except my life changed, and I had to start writing over. The notebook was no longer understandable to me. It was like it was someone else's notebook. I'd think, That looks interesting, but it doesn't interest me, it's not mine. For a long time, I thought maybe fiction was gone. I did a lot of crying about that. My desk is right across from my bed. Now, if you wrote right across from your bed, you'd wake up and say, "Oh, good, I'm going to work." And quite naturally, without even thinking about it, you'd make your coffee, do whatever you do, go to the bathroom. But, new in a wheelchair, all I could see was, I've got to dress sitting down, I've got to make the bed sitting down. I've got to wheel to the bathroom. I've got to start bringing things out to the table, I've got to do this and this before I even begin to write. Sometimes I'd get overwhelmed and I wouldn't get up. It doesn't sound like much, but a wheelchair takes a lot of physical and psychic energy. I plan everything, and it's exhausting sometimes. But I trust God. I don't always like what's coming down, but I also don't think He sends it. I hate being in a wheelchair, but I don't remember ever asking that wonderful question at the end of Bergman's *The Virgin Spring*—*Why*, God? That's an ancient question, and I've never understood it. Why would God let the atomic bomb happen? I don't know. He gives us free will. *We* let the atomic bomb happen. Sometimes we make bad choices, and sometimes things just happen that are not caused by us or by God. I read a Gospel every day, and I have learned that the ancient Jewish belief was, if things were going well, that meant that God was taking care of you. If you were crippled or poor, that meant you had brought it on yourself. I think Christ keeps saying, No, that temple didn't fall on them because they sinned. It just fell. They didn't do anything.

I come from the religion where in one verse of the Gospel, Christ says, on the cross, "My God, my God, why have you forsaken me?" And this was a wonderful thing for me to grow up with. I mean, I think if you're really a Catholic, and Catholic trained, you kind of expect to suffer.

I don't blame God for what happened to me. My faith in God is what inspired me as I was getting through it. The faith I have is a gift from Him. I know I could have turned from it, become bitter, but the way I see it, He has given me the gift of writing, and therefore, I should write. And for some reason, I got kept alive when a car hit me. I think if you're born with a soul and a gift, you're supposed to love people and use your gift.

Inspiration is a subject that we generally associate with our work and creativity, not with our hardships. But, for many people, inspiration is what moves them to re-create their lives after a loss. When Dubus prays for the Holy Spirit to be present in his life, he is asking to be filled with the Spirit that Christians believe is a gift from God. As we see in a verse from the New Testament, the gift is that "God hath sent forth the Spirit of his Son into [our] hearts" (Galatians 4:6). For those of faith, the Holy Spirit is the source of divine love, comfort, wisdom, inspiration, and healing.

That all his prayers and faith did not spare Dubus from an accident, save his leg, or save one of the people he was trying to help might lead people to ask, What good are your prayers or your faith? Taken a step further, they might also ask, What good is the God you pray to? Though Dubus did not ask the questions *Why, God?* or *Why me?* those are the first questions that many of us ask when we are faced with those freak, unreasonable things in life, which are always out there, undoing what we thought we had done with our lives and taking from us what we had. People who lose something—whether it be a leg, a child, a lover, their health—search, in their grief, for answers. Those who ordinarily have faith in God want to know what happened. Why didn't He protect them? Why were they singled out? Those who do not have faith will point to their suffering and to other hardships in the world and say, "If there was a God, this would not have taken place."

To say *Why, God?* one would have to believe that God had caused whatever had taken place. And if He hadn't actually caused it, then He was indifferent because He allowed it to happen. But why would we assume that God, the One who breathes life into our spirits, would go out of His way to cause us to suffer? Or why would He step aside, indifferently, and watch?

As Dubus himself points out, we cannot assume that our misfortunes are caused by God. "He gave us free will," he said. What this means is that He gives us the gift to make our own choices, and therefore He allows to happen whatever comes from those choices. Dubus then goes on to say, "Sometimes we make bad choices, and sometimes things just happen that are not caused by us or by God." The point is, we live in a precarious world with precarious events, which are random, erratic, and cruel at times. But why would it be God's will to disturb the order of the very thing He created? We read in Scripture that it is through God that we receive understanding, and that we receive it through His inspiration, His breath. We sense from Dubus's story, and from many others, that the breath of God will revive us, that it will fill us with enough understanding and strength to get us through the worst of hardships.

In the New Testament, Jesus took the position that suffering was not the will of God for mankind, nor did He attribute all suffering to the sins of the sufferer. However, as Dubus points out, the ancient Hebrew belief was that misfortune was a punishment for our sins and a sign of God's wrath. The ancient Hebrews were bound to one God by a covenant relationship. If the people honored God's covenant, His promise was that He would make them "a kingdom of priests, and an holy nation" (Exodus 19:6). This relationship was supposed to protect the physical, emotional, and spiritual health of the nation, on the condition that people were obedient to God's will. Since people believed that faith and obedience to God would produce physical and spiritual health, they concluded that illness and suffering were the punishment for one's transgressions for not obeying God.

However, the book of Job offers an alternate belief. In Job, disease and sin are not connected. Job shows us that a righteous person can suffer pain and can still maintain and strengthen his faith in God. It also shows us that our faith does not depend on our circumstances, nor do our circumstances depend on our faith.

If Dubus's faith depended on his circumstances, he might not be a practicing Catholic today. Would he have turned to "walking in the Lord" after being deprived of walking in the world? If we say we have faith in God when times are good, and lose all faith when times are bad, then our faith is not based on reverence or love, it is based on what we hope to receive from Him. Faith is knowing that God is there, in both the good and bad circumstances.

There are people who are survivors but not believers. They too will feel degrees of inspiration and healing, but they will look for this guidance and strength in themselves, not in God. Since human beings have limitations, and lack God's vision, we encounter these limitations as we try to heal on our own. When we struggle with anger, resentment, and pain, we might not be able to see beyond our loss, or fully let go of our grief. In Marsha Norman's play *Third and Oak,* a woman who has lost her husband talks to another woman in a Laundromat. After avoiding the subject of her husband's death, the widow tells the other woman that, in her basement, she found a beach ball that she will not throw out because it is filled with her late husband's breath.

In this remarkable image, this man is preserved. All that is left of his life is his breath. When we think of the image of the breath of God, of it being present when we are grieving, when our spirits are all but dead, we can say that it is this breath that preserves us.

Though grief cannot be measured, it has been said that none is greater than the grief one feels from the loss of a child. Monica Chusid felt both anger and grief after the death of her fifteen-month-old daughter. Chusid's daughter, Rebecca, had been hospitalized three times during her fifteen months and underwent two surgeries that doctors claimed would repair her congenital heart defect. Though heart defects in infants are sometimes serious, Chusid's doctors were optimistic that Rebecca would be fine. Each surgery was believed to have been successful, and Chusid and her husband were encouraged and relieved. "After the final surgery," Chusid said, "the doctors told my husband, Adam, and me that Rebecca had one of the best recoveries they had ever seen. We went home and relaxed. People came over and brought us food. But the next morning we were told that Rebecca had died."

Unlike Dubus, who has been a practicing Catholic and believer all of his life, Chusid, a management consultant who oversees the design and implementation of computer systems, did not turn to religion or God until after her daughter passed away.

MONICA CHUSID

After Rebecca died, one of the things that went through my mind was, Who is God and why did He do such a horrible thing to me? After sitting shiva for seven days, I went to synagogue filled with grief and anger. After the service, I said to the rabbi, "I'm sitting here, saying these prayers, these words, but I don't believe any of them." But in time, I did. In time I came to believe that God didn't do this horrible thing, that He was more like a parent who watches things happen to his children, and is there to comfort them. In trying to find some meaning in Rebecca's death, I was gaining a spiritual core. I always knew I was missing something in my life, and it was my religion and God that filled me with what I was missing. The Jewish religion has many rituals when someone dies that guide you down a pathway, and it was in going down that pathway that I began to heal.

When I was in mourning, every day I would say the Hebrew prayer, the Mourner's Kaddish. I believe that when you pray this prayer you are glorifying God's kingdom because it is not a prayer about death, it is a prayer that reaffirms life. In that seven-day period of sitting shiva, when the rabbi and congregants came to pay their respects, Adam and I would pray in the morning and evening. When that period of shiva was over, whether I could get to synagogue or not, every morning I would say the Mourner's Kaddish. I would have been lost without those rituals. They gave me a reason to get out of bed.

As I was healing, when things entered my mind that seemed to come from somewhere else, a certain kind of clarity, or wisdom, I knew that this inspiration came from my religion and from God. And, in a way that I can't fully explain, I believe that some of this inspiration came from Rebecca, that she was helping to move the wheels. Perhaps she is my messenger to God, my own personal angel. When I'm at the beach and I look at the water, I think, That's where God is, and that's where I see Rebecca. I believe she is in all things that are beautiful, and I believe that so is God.

When we think of being guided down a pathway that can help us to heal, we are reminded that healing is a process. It is a passage from one place to the next, from illness to health, from disruption to peace. For those like Chusid who have sought peace through a spiritual practice, that practice is also a process. Our prayers may seem dry and mechanical at first. We may not even believe what we are praying. But going through the motions is an act of faith. This is true, to a degree, for people of all faiths, but it is particularly consistent with the Jewish concept of inspiration, which is that through the doing comes understanding, through work comes redemption. There is not so much a focus on understanding the nature of God, but a focus, instead, on rituals. Observing rituals led Chusid down a pathway because she chose to act in faith—even before she had faith. Divine action cannot be fully at work in our lives until we open ourselves to receive it.

In the Bible, God is often seen as a parent whom we can turn to for comfort. He is Father, Creator, the giver of life. He brought Adam, the first man, to life with His breath. In the Old Testament, God is portrayed as Father of Israel: "Thus saith the Lord, Israel is my son, even my firstborn" (Exodus 4:22). In the New Testament, God is the Father of Jesus Christ. Sometimes people in the New Testament prayed to God as Abba, the Aramaic term of endearment for "father." The words "Our Father" begin the Lord's Prayer.

In comparing God to a parent, Chusid, who suffered a parent's greatest loss, knows the depth of love a parent has for a child. A parent's role is to love and care for his or her child. When a child is suffering, a parent brings comfort. But, one might say, an earthly parent does not have the power to heal; only God has the power to heal. What comfort is there when God doesn't heal a child?

To presume that all healing comes from God is to presume that if we are not healed God has abandoned us, that He deliberately or indifferently chose not to heal us. We take on the role of children who feel that God, our Father, isn't just or fair. But it is life, not God, that isn't just or fair. We have imperfect bodies, which sometimes heal and sometimes don't. We make imperfect choices that have given us an imperfect world, but God is always there. Those who believe in God's miracles do not lose faith if they don't come. God's miracles—His gifts—are mysteries. The gift of inspiration is that God fills us with understanding and vision, and enlivens our grieving spirits. Whether our bodies heal from an illness or our hearts heal from a loss, both are monumental.

There are those, like Dubus and Chusid, who believe that religious rituals bring peace and a closer sense of God, that the daily or weekly repetition of sacred acts, which are both personal and public, deepen our faith as well as our focus and commitment to God. For them, this is the essence of their healing. Yet there are those who lose someone, who do not feel drawn to organized religion, but who still find that their loss has opened for them a greater awareness of the divine. Such is the case with Mark Doty, an award-winning poet. Doty described his religious background this way: "We were Presbyterian, and sometimes we were Methodist, and when I was a teenager, my mother became an Episcopalian, and as an adolescent, I became a Roman Catholic for a while." Doty, who has published four books of poetry, writes about his loss of Wally Roberts in *Heaven's Coast,* a memoir of his life and twelve-year relationship with Roberts, who died of AIDS in 1993. In this memoir, Doty's grief is fierce, and in that grief is

God. "And I think God is *there* or, there *is* God. I know, through and through. Great grief, great God; where there is one, there is the other."[3]

MARK DOTY

There's nothing like the death of someone we love to push us toward ultimate considerations. You tend to feel like Job. You ask, If the universe is just or kind, or in any way designed, then how can what I love most be taken from me, how can this be permitted? How can the world go on and new things be coming into being when this loss seems to be sitting right in the center of everything? And my grief pushed me, as nothing else ever had, to think about these questions. That's one answer to that notion of great grief, great God—that you have no choice, in your grief, but to try to understand God in some way. I think grief is like a kind of lightning bolt; it's a force that cracks you open and shatters your sense of certainty and familiarity. Everything that had seemed ordinary and predictable to me suddenly seemed strange and unknown. Had it not been for Wally's death, I think I would have stayed in my kind of fuzzy, deist sort of spiritual thing without pushing at it too much. That loss pushed me toward an awareness of the paradoxical way in which the universe offers us the blessing of indifference. I believe, with all my heart, that God loves us profoundly, and can be utterly indifferent to us at once. It is that paradox that is right at the heart of our experience.

I found myself really drawn to think about Job. What happened to him came from this grand, indifferent, beautiful force, that whirlwind that's larger and more powerful than human life, that we can only know a little bit of. I know, as surely as I know anything, that the person who wrote the book of Job had an experience of great transformative power, and that that experience gave breath to the voice that speaks out of that whirlwind. You don't make stuff like that up. That force, that whirlwind, felt to me like a real source of consolation. *That,* I could believe. Whereas when people say he's in a better place, his suffering has ended now, you'll forget the bad stuff and you'll be left with beautiful memories, you want to say, "Oh, *please,* that doesn't speak to the kind of pain people feel." But the notion of God's power and force, the dignity and veracity of that spirit that animates the universe is something I found consolation with.

When Wally was ill, there was this extraordinary sense of feeling supported. As soon as we needed help, help was there. When I could not imagine how we were going to do what needed to be done, consistently something or someone would just appear and help us out. What I had been witness to was the worst thing that ever happened to me, and yet it was really beautiful at the same time. After Wally died, though I was miserable, I felt that I was no longer afraid to die, that the suggestion to me, from watching him, was that what happens to us as souls is something to look forward to.

Twice in this chapter we have encountered the question of whether or not God steps aside, indifferently, and watches those he loves suffer. This question has a way of stressing that God is involved in His love for us, and more incidental in our suffering than He is indifferent. However, indifference must be looked at in a different way in light of Doty's observation that what God offers us with His love is the *"blessing* of indifference."

To think of God as indifferent, we might presume that He is uncaring, but to speak of God's love is to imply that God cares. Yet, when we do use the word *indifferent* to describe God in terms of the role He plays in our suffering, what we end up with is a neutral God—but neutral in regard to what? Many people have felt that God is not absent from our hardships, but that He waits out those hardships with us, loving us. This act of waiting, of supporting us as we are suffering, implies that God is not neutral when it comes to *us,* but that He is without preference when it comes to our process, to how long our suffering lasts, because He sees beyond our suffering before He inspires us to. He knows that healing is at work, that good can come out of anything. This is the blessing of indifference—that God, with all His force and love, may care less about our grief than what is beyond it.

God's Spirit, the *ruach,* forcefully proceeds as breath from God's mouth—like a whirlwind, as Doty puts it. Those who say that they have been filled with inspiration in their work and creativity have experienced a whirlwind of productivity, but the work itself seemed to have been given to them, to have passed through them more in the sense of a whisper than a whirlwind, as if they were vessels that were filled with a quality of work that was beyond what they felt they could take credit for. The whirlwind in our suffering is the suffering itself, which fights against the peace that, at the same time, is healing us. We do not always know that this peace is there. At first we may not see it, or feel it, or recognize it. But in our spirits, God's Spirit is already at work. We will come to feel it if we leave an opening. And in the same way that inspiration produces a quality of work that we cannot fully credit to ourselves, inspiration also produces a quality of peace, a new level of understanding, an intense degree of love and resilience that seems like a gift from the divine, from somewhere beyond us.

Wherever "beyond" us is, it is not only the place where God is; somewhere beyond us is the destination for the souls of those who die. There are so many unresolved details about what happens to us when we die—whether we maintain our identities, where we will go, and whether or not we will be with God. Many people have sensed, when they watch someone die, that the soul of this suffering person is now at peace and passing from one place to the next. During our conversation, Mark Doty told us that when he watched Wally die, "he seemed to me to just fly out of his body. It was as if he had leapt up, and I have the image in my head of him sort of somersaulting up and out, through the wall and out of that room into the next thing." Those who have had near-death experiences have reported that, for an instant, they have actually been guided by what appears to be God, or an angel, or someone they loved who had died, that they were being taken to some place beyond this world. Throughout the New Testament, Jesus offers believers the promise of heaven as a place where the suffering will end, where with Him they will receive transformed bodies and glorious, eternal life.

As healing is a passage from one place to the next, so is birth. At birth we cross the threshold from *not* being in this world to being in this world, and after living our lives, there is the passage from life to death. For those who have found that inspiration and healing are gifts that come from beyond us, it would make sense that the thought of our souls passing from here to beyond here, to the source of those gifts, would bring comfort. When Doty said that in watching someone die he was no longer afraid to die, he helps us see that this can be a turning point in one's faith. Faith is the antithesis of fear. Inspiration often comes in the form of a revelation that moves us to see something differently, or to do something differently. What was not clear to us suddenly becomes clear and, depending on our circumstances, will then have an impact on our work, or our faith, or our healing.

For many, to see death up close is life-changing. We talked about this with Diana Eck. Professor Eck grew up in Bozeman, Montana, with a Methodist background, and lived there until she moved east to attend Smith College. During her junior year at Smith, Eck traveled to India, to the city of Banaras. "I wanted to go somewhere that was very different from the kind of middle-class European American culture that I had known," Eck said. "Everything about the Hindu tradition was a surprise for me, something I needed to wrestle with and think about. There were so many pilgrims, so many worshipers, so many temples, so many gods, and so much to learn, almost nothing of which I already knew." As a practicing Christian, Eck maintains that her faith has been strengthened by her relationships to people of other faiths. She spoke about this when she talked about her brother, who died as a result of injuries he sustained in a jail in Mexico, where he had been held without charges. She credited the way she faced his death, and the way she has faced death in general, to the faith she developed as a Christian in dialogue with Hindus when she lived in India.

DIANA ECK

My brother was in one sense murdered. He probably had internal injuries that he didn't realize the extent of until it was too late. He died alone in a little hospital in Juárez, and then was taken to a warehouse-type place that was the morgue. Going to the storefront doctor's office, going to the hotel he had stayed in, going to the hospital where he had died, going to the morgue where he was and identifying his body—all of that was extremely difficult. Yet to claim his death and claim his life, and also to claim a faith that doesn't run away from death but stands with death, was very, very important for me. Christian faith does not run away from death. I think that's true of all the world's great religious traditions, that death is part of them. I may have been able to cultivate that kind of faith better because of my experience in India. I lived in Banaras, a place that was a city of death, where Hindus come to die and be cremated and have their ashes committed to the waters of the Ganges. I had never really seen death up close until I went to Banaras as a twenty-year-old. Literally, every time I went to town, even if I went on a happy mission to buy sweets for a party, I was likely to encounter a funeral party carrying a corpse to the cremation grounds. And the cremation grounds weren't hidden off in some secret part of the city. They were visible, present, part of the ongoing swirl of life in the city. The inextricable relation of life and death is inescapable in a city like Banaras. In a way, it is inescapable in the Hindu tradition because the visible representations of the divine often include the horrific things we would associate with death—skulls, for example. This makes one realize that God is present not only in light and life and joy, but that the presence of God abides in death and suffering as well.

In the Christian tradition, it is so very clear to me that God accompanies us in our suffering. I see the Christian story as a story of accompaniment—that God so loved the world that God became one of us and accompanies us. God accompanies us not just in our life, and in the challenges of growth, but God accompanies us in the sorrow, in the suffering, in the confronting of illness and death and tragedy that are also part of the fabric of our lives. They're part of everyone's life. We can't see those moments as somehow outside the providence of God, or as provocation for us to say, If God were really on the job, we would be shielded from those times, or God would remove those times from us. God is present right in the midst of those times. I think that is the power of the Christian story.

God does not shield us from life. In fact, Jesus tells us in the Gospel of John that in this world we will have trials. There will be suffering and there will be death. "But be of good cheer," Jesus says; "I have overcome the world" (John 16:33).

God so loved the world, and it is this love that overcomes the world. Jesus himself was not spared suffering or death, and He suffered and died because God loved the world. We do not have to see or understand the presence of God to know that it is fully there. "Yea, though I walk through the valley of the shadow of death, I will fear no evil: for thou art with me" (Psalm 23:4). God, in all valleys, is with us.

God does not shield us from life, and life is not shielded from God. He is often the first thing we relect on when life fills us with despair. This is true of believers and nonbelievers. When our suffering pushes us to reflect on God, this is an act that often leads us toward humility and surrender. During our conversation with author Rick Moody, he said, "I can't think of myself as a powerful entity. I think of myself as someone who is trying to get my will in line with God's will for me." Moody, who has published the novels *Purple America, The Ice Storm,* and *Garden State,* a collection of stories, and co-edited the nonfiction anthology *Joyful Noise: The New Testament Revisited,* prays before he works. He attends an Episcopal church, "pretty regularly, a couple of times a month." His spiritual search began after he was hospitalized for a nervous breakdown while in his twenties.

The night before we were scheduled to meet with Moody, he called to reschedule. His thirty-seven-year-old sister, who had had no previous medical condition, had passed away unexpectedly. With no warning, her heart had stopped. Moody was canceling just about every social and work-related appointment at that time, but he told us that he wanted to meet with us. He felt that talking about spiritual issues would be healing.

RICK MOODY

I always write in the mornings. I believe that whole Thoreauvian thing that to be awake is to be alive, that sunrise is important. So that's when I do my work, with that idea of inspiration. Yet, at the same time, I can find the solitariness of late nights really beautiful, and that's a time when I feel that I'm in a larger arc of creation. I don't rely on myself or my own sense of power to try to accomplish things in life, and in the universe.

I have been hospitalized for mental illness, for what they sometimes call clinical depression, and it seems that the only reason I'm functioning is because I'm supposed to function in a certain way, and that part of my job as a writer is testamentary to a strength that is broader and more complicated than my own. I had a nervous breakdown in the eighties, when I was twenty-five, and I recovered from it, and I haven't had a relapse. I tried all the normal Western medical treatments, but what helped me was recognizing some kind of spiritual yearning in myself. I had that sense of estrangement and isolation that comes from feeling that I was out there forging in the world for my own, for whatever I could get. I started to want to be a part of God, and of community.

I didn't have a white-light conversion experience. I never woke up one morning and said, "Damn, I'm lucky to have God," and went out and tried to convert other people to this cause. In fact, I came kicking and screaming. In the first years after I got out of the hospital, one day I would seek God, and the next day I wouldn't. I felt that my training as a sort of deconstructionist lit-crit guy was entirely opposed to all of this, and that I would never be able to swallow it. In graduate school, at Columbia University, where I was just before all of this happened, I had this reputation for being excessively cerebral, and not understanding emotional things at all. Back then, I was thinking about fiction like it was a crossword puzzle, and not like it was an explication of human feelings or the human spirit. I'm not sure I would have been able to think about fiction differently unless I had gone through a spiritual search. Once I started looking to God, my life improved, and a lot of the troubles I had as a younger person just weren't troubling anymore.

The only thing that I can attribute this to is grace, that God gave me a gift during those troubling times that was completely unwarranted, but it came nonetheless. Flannery O'Connor uses this idea of grace in the sense that the least noteworthy, appropriate people are, occasionally, granted these gifts, that no matter what they have done with their lives, something comes along to change everything. In my case, it was the gift of peace.

Recently, I have been thinking a lot about where I stand in terms of God. My sister died, really suddenly and unexpectedly. Her heart just stopped. She was thirty-seven, quite young and vital, and she has two kids who already went through a difficult divorce. In a situation like this, I don't think you can help but ask, if you're a believing person, what on earth is God's will, if God's will is to drastically upset the lives of these two children, not to mention my life, my brother's, and my parents'. My cousin, who is a minister, said, "God doesn't do these things, but God lets these things happen." And that seems to be one explanation. But prior to this time, my idea was that God's will for me was to be happy, joyous, and free. And I don't understand right now how I'm supposed to be happy about this. But I can't help feeling, as I usually do, that bereft is closest to God. Like right now, more than any other time in the last year or so, I go around and, in this emptiness, in this sense of loss, I feel *more* like there's a God rolling around in the heavens. And that seems overwhelming. They say Jesus wept at Lazarus' grave. Jesus knew what the afterlife was all about, and yet, a friend of His died, and He wept. I can't help but feel that earthly sorrow is a part of life, and there's no way around it. It's horrible, and it has been painful dealing with it, but it doesn't contradict a belief in God.

I have been writing about my sister these last two weeks. I didn't feel that I was capable of making a narrative or making any kind of structure for these remarks. I just turned on the computer and let my memory flow without trying to corral it in any way. So I was making these little chunks, these little paragraphs without trying to organize them in any fashion. And this morning, I woke—I always do my best thinking when I refuse to get out of bed—and I started thinking about my sister; she was a photographer, and what I realized was that the little chunks were themselves snapshots, and that just by not organizing, by letting myself be guided in some way, I had found the perfect vehicle to try and address her memory.

Ever since my focus has been on God, I have been much more engaged in writing about human consciousness and spiritual issues. Especially right now, going through what I'm going through, it seems to me that if fiction isn't dealing with life or death issues, and really trying to deal with the spirit in some way, it's not doing its job. The whole process for me of becoming and being spiritual has come from a relentless experience with humility—plans going awry, and all my ideas about how my life was supposed to turn out being obliterated by fate. I believe that God locates Himself at the spot where you recognize your own fallibility and your neediness. And the paradox of it all has been that whenever I give up, like I am trying to do now, I seem to do better.

Surrender. It seems to happen every time. The moment we come to the point of feeling that we can no longer meet our challenge—that we give up, that we are not invested anymore in doing it our way, apart from seeking God's way—it is in this raw, open, humble place that we leave an opening for God to inspire us. He will help us not to give up, but to get up and begin again—without being attached to a particular outcome.

Nonbelievers may consider it weakness to say, I can't do this by myself, without God. Their advice would be to look to ourselves for strength. The inside strength that nonbelievers look to is will, but if our will is not in line with God's will, with his larger vision, then we may only come up with temporary solutions and comfort. When Rick Moody talks about having had "a relentless experience with humility—plans going awry, and all my ideas about how my life was supposed to turn out being obliterated by fate," we are reminded that life does not always cooperate with our will and our vision. Our real strength comes from having the courage to surrender our plans and to ask God to fill us with His.

Moody's explanation as to why his life improved when he started looking to God is—grace. The free and unearned gift of God. Grace is God's unconditional gift of mercy and assistance that blesses our lives. Though we may be fallible, weak, or undeserving, God's grace is a gift, and is given entirely apart from merit.

It is usually when we are fallible and weak that we turn to God in prayer. As personal as our prayers for healing are, they are also, often, public. Many people feel led to pray with others in small groups, or in congregations. In addition to churches and synagogues, there are ministries at work. During our interview with Gary Carter, an eleven-time all-star baseball player, and currently a television sports commentator, he talked about how he now serves as president of Baseball Chapel, an organization that provides ministry to ballplayers.

GARY CARTER

Baseball players go on road trips, and this can be very disruptive in one's life. I have seen broken marriages, alcoholism, drug addiction, and financial collapse. The main purpose of the Baseball Chapel is to minister to ballplayers if they are searching or hurting or healing from something. It is available to every player on every team. Usually there is a chapel leader on each team who rounds up the players for a chapel service. The service may last only ten or fifteen minutes. It's an opportunity to pray, to hear a message from the Bible, and to listen to the testimonies of ex-ballplayers, ex-inmates, or to someone who might have made a strong impact, whose life has changed because of God. Because they listened to the voice of God. It's not a matter of going around with a Bible and hitting players over the head with it, or preaching to them, or anything like that. It's really for the players to be able to fellowship together, to attend Bible studies together, to see how God has had an impact on people's lives, and how much more of an impact these people can then have on someone else's life.

I felt that God really guided me in this direction to do this work, to be there for other ballplayers. During my first year in spring training, I had a roommate who shared Scripture with me. He suggested that I bring Jesus into my life. As soon as I did, my life changed. I felt more peace and strength than ever before. This changed me for the better as a human being, and as a ballplayer. I decided then that I was going to do everything that I could to have an impact on others. I wanted to give something back.

I'll never forget when Bob Costas interviewed me after the Mets won the 1986 World Series. There was all this jubilation in the clubhouse, and what I wound up saying when Bob asked me how I felt was "I just want to give all the praise and glory to Jesus." Now I know that there are a lot of entertainers and athletes who are believers, who are reluctant to bring up any words of acknowledgment toward God because maybe they'll be ridiculed or sound weak. But I don't care what anyone says. I get my strength and inspiration from God. I have always found, and I tell the other ballplayers, that God has a way of pointing out to us, when we try to face any challenge without seeking Him, that, hey, if you just let me help out and be a part of it, then your life will be a lot calmer and a lot simpler.

It might seem surprising that a group of baseball players would sit together before a Sunday game and pray for themselves and each other. But Gary Carter told us that there are organized ministries not just for baseball, but also for professional athletes who play hockey, football, and basketball, and whose lives have changed, according to Carter, "because they listened to the voice of God." There are many voices in the world in addition to God's voice. There are the voices of people who disappoint and deceive us. There is our own critical voice, which discourages us. And there is evil. This is the voice that misleads us the most because we do not always recognize its darkness. All of these voices drain us. None of them make our lives simpler or inspire us. Ministries like Baseball Chapel, through prayer, help to fill our spirits after the other voices have emptied us.

There are practices that bring people peace and healing other than prayer, such as meditation and various relaxation techniques. Certain studies have shown that these practices are more effective when done in a context of faith. We can see this in the studies of Dr. Herbert Benson, M.D. Benson is a physician, and president and founder of Harvard University's Mind/Body Medical Institute in Boston. He is the author of several books, including *Timeless Healing: The Power and Biology of Belief.* For over twenty-five years he has researched the healing benefits of affirming beliefs, particularly beliefs in a higher power. His work, he said, "is really the scientific exploration of divine inspiration." His studies have shown that people have received hope, strength, and healing from prayer, and from other practices of belief. At the Mind/Body Institute, Benson and his colleagues offer a variety of techniques that aim to bring forth what Benson calls "the relaxation response." According to these studies, the people who said that they felt an increased sense of spirituality and peace from "the relaxation response" reported that they felt the presence of God's Spirit—a Spirit that they recognized was beyond themselves. As a result, Benson said that it was these people whose health improved the most.

HERBERT BENSON, M.D.

Our work has evolved over twenty-five to thirty years, and it has been focused on how the mind interacts with the body. We initially defined that if you thought in a certain way and had a repetition of a word, a sound, a prayer, and passively disregarded other thoughts, that a physiological state evolved that was opposite to the stress state. We call that physiologic state *the relaxation response,* which is opposite to the so called stress-related fight-or-flight response. We also came to recognize that the most profound belief among many people is a belief in God. And that led to the reasoning that showed that belief in God, in an infinite absolute, can often lead to healing. There hasn't been a culture of human beings that has not invoked a belief in God, in forces, in something lasting beyond our time. And it is in that sense that one sees that this image of God has always been there as long as humans have been thinking. One could argue that we are even wired for God. According to a 1990 Gallup poll, 95 percent of Americans say that they believe in God, and that speaks to this being perhaps the most important belief system they have. In our teachings, we have seen that prayer often evokes the physiological changes of the relaxation response. When I give my patients a choice of utilizing a word, or sound, or a prayer, 80 percent will choose a prayer.

�֎

In speaking with Walter Levine, a survivor since 1989 of multiple myeloma, a form of bone cancer, who had originally been given three days to live, he said that the first thing he recommends to others who have cancer is to pray. Levine said that when he asked God why he survived, God answered, "I kept you around to help people."

Sometimes we are used by God as instruments of assistance in other people's lives; sometimes He uses us to inspire others. And Levine has been used as an instrument of assistance in the lives of many people.

Since his recovery from cancer, Levine, a highly successful business entrepreneur, makes himself available to cancer patients from around the world, who call him and write to him asking for guidance in how they too can survive. In addition to giving inspiration to cancer patients, Levine and his wife have been at the heart of fund-raising and volunteering for and supporting various organizations, including Norwalk Connecticut's Lower Fairfield Center, a state-subsidized home for the retarded. Levine's son, one of his four children, is a resident there. The Levine family's annual fund-raising events also help to support other group homes for the mentally retarded, as well as the Westport Alcoholism and Drug Dependency Council.

In both the advice he gives to cancer patients and in his work with retarded children and adults, Levine places a priority on the healing power of prayer. Levine, who is Jewish, arranged to have a private meeting with Mother Teresa and the residents of Lower Fairfield Center in 1996, so that Mother Teresa would say a prayer for them and offer divine direction. "When she touched me," Levine told us, "I knew that I was touched by God in some way."

WALTER LEVINE

When I was diagnosed with multiple myeloma, the doctors in New York gave me three days to live. And, of course, I found that silly because it was a purely educated guess. I was in the hospital, on my back, and I couldn't move. I had just crushed my vertebrae and three discs. That's how they found the cancer. I fell on the tennis court. So I didn't go anywhere, I just prayed. You don't have to go anywhere to talk to God. You don't need a church and you don't need a temple. If you don't believe that He's with you at all times, you don't believe. Even when your prayers aren't answered right away. That year I went through twenty-five chemotherapies. They burned out all of my bone marrow. After the last chemotherapy, the doctor said, "You're fine," so my wife and I went down to Puerto Rico and celebrated. When I came back and went for a test, I still had the same percentage of cancer in my body. I went in with 93 percent cancer, and even with all of those treatments, I came out with 93 percent cancer. When I confronted my doctor, he put me in touch with the Arkansas Cancer Research Center. They have done wonderful things with multiple myeloma. Dr. Bart Barlogie is the number-one cancer specialist in the world, and he's there. So I went, and I was one of the first cancer patients to have a stem cell transplant. Today it's fairly common. And here I am. I survived.

Hundreds of cancer patients have called me on the telephone— from South Africa, from Australia, from the Caribbean, from every part of the world that I could imagine. I talk to everyone who calls me, and I tell them this: There are certain things that can be done. I tell them exactly what I do. Number one on the list is prayer. You have to have a lot of prayer, support from your family and your friends, great medicine—I take sea cucumber from Australia, I take enzymes, I take liver pills, I take multivitamins, I take a chromium pill—you have to exercise, have a sense of humor, and a positive attitude, which is faith. I have asked God, "What on earth did you keep me around for?" and the answer came back suddenly. He said, "I kept you around to help people." Well, my wife and I have been doing work with retarded children and adults for thirty-seven years. We've also done work on behalf of alcohol and drug abuse, and now cancer. I'm doing what He asked.

And then I had something to ask. I have a son who is retarded, who is a resident with other residents in a place in Norwalk, and I asked if Mother Teresa would pray for them. The reason the whole thing began was because I received a call from Bernadette Coomaraswamy, who for twenty-five years had been Mother Teresa's lawyer and personal advisor in the United States. She called because her husband, Rama, has the same cancer that I had. I put Rama in touch with Dr. Barlogie in Arkansas, and now he's being treated by him and getting well. Then Bernadette called me one day and asked if there was anything that she could do for me. I said, no, not for me, but one of the retarded children had recently died, and I said, "If Mother Teresa is ever in the United States, I would appreciate it if she would say a prayer for the children, with the children." Bernadette sent a letter to Mother Teresa that said, "There is a dedicated man who has the same disease as Rama. He and his wife have done great work with the retarded children and adults in our area. There is a particular place in neighboring Norwalk that is in special need of your prayers. I know that if God so arranges it, you may yet come, but you will know what to do."

Eventally, I received, by personal messenger, a note from Mother Teresa. It said, "Dear Walter, I am sorry to hear about your sickness. Accept your affliction as a gift from God. It is hard, but the wood of the cross was hard too. Do not be afraid. Jesus loves you with an everlasting love. I am praying much for you and the people you serve.

May his passion shared with you be a sign of his tender love, and through it grow in his likeness, and be an instrument of his compassion for the suffering people you come across. God bless you, Mother Teresa."

So that's the way it happened. When she came to the United States, to a Roman Catholic church in the Bronx, my wife and I brought three of the children to the Mass for a blessing. Mother Teresa spent twenty minutes with us. There was a depth in that lady's eyes that I have never seen before in any human being.

God is a forgiving, merciful God, but life isn't merciful. In life you're put through tests. I have three healthy children, and one retarded son. Why? I had cancer and was given three days to live. Why? God didn't cause my cancer. My stupidity of smoking and not knowing what I was doing as a child helped my cancer. I don't think God is an angry God. If you believe that He'll help you, He'll help you. I think that 99 percent of everything you do in life is attitude. If you have a relationship with God and you've got the right attitude, you're not afraid of Him. I have learned how to ask one question in life that covers everything, and that question is this: How can I help you?

The will to live, to succeed, and to do God's will involves both persistence and surrender. As Levine understands well, only to know of God's power is not enough. In order to do the will of God, we must be in motion if He is to guide us. Whatever He wants to accomplish for us, He does *through* us, not *for* us. In all of Levine's challenges, he never stopped moving. He never stayed bitter, self-focused, or beaten down. His focus was on God, even during his recovery from what he was told was "incurable" cancer. Levine has chosen to rise from all of his challenges by living a life of love and service. Service to God, who has inspired him, and service to others, whom he inspires.

When Levine says of Mother Teresa that "When she touched me, I knew I was touched by God in some way," we are given the sense of how close to God are the people who minister to others through prayer. They are the vessels through which He inspires, comforts, and offers divine direction. And when *we* pray, we are the vessels through which, at times, through grace He inspires. Prayer is to the soul what breathing is to the body. It gives our spirits life, sustenance, and healing.

REVELATION

BEFORE AND AFTER

Faith is the word that describes the direction our feet start moving when we find that we are loved. Faith is stepping out into the unknown with nothing to guide us but a hand just beyond our grasp.[1]

FREDERICK BUECHNER,
The Magnificent Defeat

As the story goes, Saint Paul (who was then called Saul) was on his way to Damascus to persecute the Christians, when "suddenly a light from heaven flashed around him. He fell to the ground and heard a voice say to him, 'Saul, Saul, why do you persecute me?'

" 'Who are you, Lord?' Saul said.

" 'I am Jesus, whom you are persecuting,' he replied. 'Now get up and go into the city, and you will be told what you must do' " (Acts 9:3–6—NIV).

Then Saul got up from the ground.

The question for many people is, How did he fall down?

They do not mean how did the light from heaven make him fall down but, in a much more technical way, from where did he fall?

Some say that Paul fell off his horse, but the Bible makes no mention of a horse. Another possibility is that he had been walking to Damascus, and when he "saw the light" he fell.

In an article written by Charles T. Dougherty, he said that after being a professor of English for thirty-seven years, and describing, in lectures, Paul being knocked off his horse by this light, he learned from one of his students that the Bible makes no mention of a horse. He believes that the difference in perception "flows from the fact that Catholics are brought up in the presence of religious art, especially the paintings of the Italian Renaissance, and Protestants are not."[2] According to Dougherty, the Renaissance artists saw Paul as an important man, and men of importance rode horses. Because these artists painted Paul on a horse, this is what the Catholics saw.

This is only one interpretation, he concedes, and explains it further by saying that Catholicism has been around for longer than the printed word, and without the printed word, artwork was what people looked to for information and contemplation. Protestantism was formed later, when printed Bibles were available. Pictures, as tools for teaching, were no longer necessary.

I find it interesting that this detail of how Paul traveled to Damascus—by horse or by foot—would be so important and so unimportant at the same time in the context of Paul's revelation and conversion. The conversion, of course, is the point, not whether Paul walked or rode a horse. However, where we are, who we are, what we are doing at the exact moment that we receive a revelation is significant in this sense: we are someone doing something before the revelation, and we are a different someone afterward. Knowing details like whether we were on a horse or on our feet when this change occurred helps us to remember who we no longer are.

Paul was guided, inspired, and empowered by God through revelation. He was blinded for three days, so that when his sight was restored, his old vision was replaced with new vision. He could see the God that he had not before seen. Divine revelation enables us to see beyond our human, limited capacities. We can then step into the unknown, knowing that God has given us a new purpose in life, and that God is guiding our steps.

Revelation involves being inspired by the Spirit of God to see something differently and to do something differently. Unlike Saint Paul, most of us do not hear God's voice as if it were a human sound, but His Spirit is at work in our vision, our thinking, our actions, and our hearts, guiding, inspiring, and empowering us to express the divine nature through our lives and our work.

We can see revelation at work in the lives of people in all circumstances. Whether the revelation comes through Scripture, or through a private revelation that stops us from continuing on the path we are on, there is always an awakening.

When talking with gospel singer Helen Baylor, she spoke about how a revelation that she received entirely redirected her life. After years of alcohol and drug addiction, Helen Baylor emerged from obscurity in 1991 to become one of gospel music's leading performing artists. Her 1994 album, *The Live Experience,* held the number-one spot on the Contemporary Christian music charts for months. Even as the demands of her successful recording and performing career increase, Baylor still devotes considerable time to Baylor Ministries, which was formed to help those in prisons, in homes for unwed mothers, and in urban areas where there is poverty, sickness, and drug addiction.

This is who she is now, but Baylor was very candid about who she used to be.

When she was thirteen years old, she began performing as an opening act for established rhythm and blues artists. When she was sixteen, she gave birth to a baby she could not care for, and by the time she was eighteen, she was addicted to pills and cocaine. After being addicted to drugs for over a decade, Baylor found herself alone one night, drunk and high, flipping through the channels on her television until she came upon a Christian program. Baylor talked about the revelation that she had that night, and about the path that her life has taken since then.

HELEN BAYLOR

When I was a child, I used to go to church and watch people worship the Lord. I would listen to the preacher and the choir, and I knew that God was real. By the time I was nine years old, my faith was strong. But two years later, I moved with my parents to California, and I didn't get to go to church anymore, because my parents didn't go. Eventually, I stopped thinking about church and about God. When I was twelve, I started singing in nightclubs, and by the time I was thirteen I was the opening act for people like Aretha Franklin, B. B. King, and Stevie Wonder. That was a lot of fun, and really exciting. I joined the cast of the Broadway musical *Hair* when I was seventeen. My mother and father had given me permission to join the touring company by signing some kind of waiver, and I toured with the cast until I was almost twenty years old. I then went on to sing in bands, and to do background singing for different groups like the Captain & Tennille, and Chaka Khan.

A year before I toured with *Hair,* I had a baby. I spent time—a very devastating time—in a home for unwed mothers. When I got the opportunity to join the cast of *Hair,* travel, and make a lot of money, I really wanted to escape the situation and the responsibility of having a child. I didn't know how to take care of a baby, so my son went to live with my parents. That year, when I was in *Hair,* I became addicted to alcohol, pills, and cocaine, and I remained addicted for about twelve years. I had come very close to overdosing on cocaine a couple of times. During that time, I was never really happy. I let people walk all over me—that is, if I wasn't walking all over them. I had no hope, because I felt I had no future, nothing to wake up for in the morning. Then one night, like many other nights, I figured I might as well drink myself to sleep, so I started drinking and smoking and getting high. I was flipping through the channels on TV, in the living room of my little dinky apartment in North Hollywood, California, and a Christian television show got my attention. As I watched it, it became more and more apparent to me what kind of condition I was in. It was like I was seeing myself going downhill for the first time. I said to God, "Please take me back, set me free of this lifestyle,

I'm tired of living like this and being like this." And in the most incredible, merciful, unbelievable way, I experienced an instant deliverance. From that moment on, I actually lost my desire for alcohol and drugs. This is so hard to convey, but it happened. I was a walking dead woman before that night, and all of a sudden, I could feel God's presence, and I felt alive. I felt free. I felt something that I hadn't felt in years—happy. I felt the way I did when I was nine years old, when I believed so strongly in God. He was filling me with inspiration. I no longer desired the things that I medicated myself with, I only desired to know Him.

Before this night, I had tried other paths that I thought would lead to peace. I went to a place where I would sit on the floor, look at fruit, smell incense, and chant. I tried that; it didn't work. I had tried reading all kinds of books, and I had even dabbled in the occult. I had tried all the things that other people said would work. If someone would say, Take a candle, light it, say something three times, ring a bell—whatever it was, I would try it. But it wasn't until I called upon the name of Jesus, out of a pure heart wanting to be free, that things changed. That night, the revelation was, I once was lost, but now I'm found. Old things truly passed away. No, not all my bills were paid, not all of my problems were gone, and I still looked the same except that my countenance was brighter and had new life. But I was alive, and before this night I was dead. And only God could do this.

Another significant thing that happened was that my desire for singing had changed. I no longer wanted to sing secular music. I just wanted to sing gospel music. I believed that God was going to use my voice for His glory. Now, I thought that He was going to make me the next Mahalia Jackson within six months, but He didn't. I started working for the church, and I sat in the church for six years before I sang professionally again. I started out duplicating tapes at six dollars an hour. And then my job was to read thousands and thousands of letters written to the pastor. I would read this mail and route it to different departments. I went to church every Sunday, then I would go to work, make my six dollars an hour, tithe part of it, and then go to choir rehearsal. It was years before I was even asked to sing a solo with the choir. That was very frustrating, especially when people would ask me questions like "Didn't you use to sing with Chaka Khan?"

But during those six years, I had gotten married and had children. I had also spent those years studying the Bible, and there is nothing like the Bible. I believe that every question we have in life can be answered on those pages. I learned about character and integrity, and about things that I needed to know in order to do what I'm doing now.

It was when I finally said to God, "Whether or not I ever sing another note, I am still going to serve you," that things began to open up for me. All of a sudden, out of nowhere, people began to give my husband and me money. People that we didn't even know. A thousand dollars, two thousand dollars, three thousand dollars. By then I had been singing at funerals and weddings at the church, so people would hear my voice and then hand me money so that I could make a tape. I eventually recorded a four-song cassette. Someone took it to a radio station in Los Angeles, and the station began to play it on the air. Bookstores began to call our house and say, "Can you bring us ten or fifteen or twenty of those cassettes?" Then a distributor called me and said, "You know, I don't know who you are, but I would love to distribute your cassette because we're getting a lot of calls for your music." Eventually, my songs reached the top of the charts in L.A. One day, on my way to Bible study, I walked into this distributor's office with boxes of cassettes to sell him, and there was a man there from Word Records. He wanted to set up an interview with me. I eventually signed with Word Records without ever sending out a tape, or a picture, or a résumé. I attribute all of this to God. I believe that everything was moving by His Spirit.

Now when I sing, I just stand there and say, "God, I am your vessel. Use me the way you want to." That is when God uses me in the greatest way. There is a song that I sing called "Look a Little Closer." I wrote this song because I wanted to say, "Look at me. Can you see that I have changed? If you look closely, you'll know that there is a God. He helped me, and He can help you, too." I try to encourage people in my concerts, and use my experiences to let people know that whatever it is that they are going through, there is hope.

When I became a Christian, the son I gave birth to before I was married was twelve years old. I wanted him to live with my husband and me, but by then he was attached to my parents. Also he was angry with me, and didn't want to live with me. Now he is in his late twenties, and he lives five minutes away from me. We're the best of friends. In the last couple of years, we have worked through the hurt. But one of the things in my life that I regret the most is that I didn't raise him, that I didn't have the sense to get off drugs and take care of my son. But I'm grateful for the grace of God, and the inspiration He gave me to go on, to forgive myself, and to be forgiven.

God directs our steps, but He also puts desires in our hearts. No matter what I desire now, I want to make sure that I hear from God, and that I am where He wants me to be, when He wants me to be there. God's grace is sufficient to help us face our problems. Even if the problems that we have never seem to go away, we have the grace of God to endure.

Sometimes we can receive a revelation and gain clarity in an instant. Something is revealed to us and, suddenly, we see. For those who see instantly, what precedes and follows each revelation is what takes time. Revelation is divine communication that can stop us in our tracks, and then lead us to another path, which will take time to follow.

However, we do not always see instantly. Though revelation may be that point in between the path before and after, we often see, learn, and digest things in stages. God could flash a message to us in neon lights, and we might take in only part of His message, or choose to walk away from it entirely. How many times have we known in our hearts something that is true, and then chose not to listen to our hearts?

We spend the majority of our lives in process, going through different stages and changes, reflecting on what we see. We all do not experience the instant deliverance that Baylor did, even if we receive an instant revelation. We may still desire our old way of life, whether that life is right for us or not. It takes inspiration to empower us to walk away from what we knew, to change our focus from our old life to God. And even when we do, we then begin a new process of living a different kind of life.

Every process and every stage involves reflection, and it is ironic that we tend to take more time with small details than we do with the weightier matters of our lives. We can take forever discussing the qualities we are looking for in a prospective spouse, and forever going over in our minds how we have acted toward each potential spouse, and how he or she has acted toward us. But when it comes to the heart of the matter, when the person reveals the most intimate part of his or her character, when we realize that we are in love, we no longer get obsessed about how we may or may not be right for each other, or whether we have faith in this person or not. We are stopped dead in our tracks with our heart beating the answer. We no longer process at that moment, we choose. We have the chance passionately, spontaneously to reorient our lives. To a different degree, this is what happens when God reveals His intimate Spirit to us. We are stopped dead in our tracks. We choose. We are willing to reorient our lives or we are not.

As we have seen with Baylor, revelation takes place when God reveals something to us about our lives and about His Spirit. Once

God reveals Himself to us, once He enlivens our spirits, we can then reflect His Divine Spirit to others. Baylor is able to do this through her music. The artist Howard Finster had a revelation that now allows him to do this through his art.

Howard Finster is a world-renowned folk artist who lives in Summerville, Georgia. Much of Finster's work falls under the category "sacred art" in that not only are his subjects religious in nature, but they often include Scripture.

In 1961, Finster began his creation of Paradise Gardens, located in his hometown of Summerville. Paradise Gardens is a maze of sculptures and structures, with the pervasive presence of Scriptures, their lessons, and Finster's "messages" from God. Thousands of visitors come to Paradise Gardens each year, making it one of Georgia's top-ten tourist attractions.

For much of his life, Finster worked as a Baptist preacher, and supported his wife and five children by taking on various side jobs that utilized his self-learned skills in carpentry, painting, plumbing, and mechanical repair. His constant search for a profession that could support his family while giving him ample opportunity to preach the Word of God finally manifested itself through a divine revelation, which he described to us during our interview. This revelation, which occurred when Finster was sixty years old, led him into his career as a folk artist.

HOWARD FINSTER

In 1929, when I was thirteen years old, I went to an altar call at a revival meeting that was held in an old schoolhouse. It was an altar call for people to come and pray to God. I was under conviction that night, and I wanted a change in my life and in my spirit. When I went to the altar, all I could say was "O, God, save my soul." That was all I knew how to say, and that was all that needed to be said. So I prayed and prayed. And the Holy Spirit came into my life, and lifted my soul up, and made a new person out of me that night. That was the greatest thing that happened in all the days of my life. When I walked out that old schoolhouse door, and I looked into the sky that night, the heavens just shined, and the stars looked different. They were the brightest stars that I had ever seen. I had been born to the Holy Ghost, the Holy Spirit of God. And that is still with me now, and I am over eighty years old. It will never leave me, that feeling of the Holy Ghost.

I believe that God's Spirit called me to create sacred art. I was at a university in Miami, and I was showing a slide of my work on the screen and talking about it, and there was a moment when I felt that God was saying to me, "Howard, you're teaching in a big university, and you only have an eighth-grade education. How did you get here? You're talking about Scripture in this university, and it is against the law to even have prayer in this place." I believe that the only reason I was there was because of God, because of His purpose for me. God doesn't only call wise people or educated people to do His work. In the Bible, He often inspired simple people.

I was inspired to do sacred art when I was fixing a bicycle. I used to repair bicycles for poor kids—I fixed anything that people wanted me to fix—and one day I was painting something on one of those bicycles and I found out I couldn't patch it the way I wanted to using a little brush. It left marks, so I reached over and it felt like something told me, "Just take your finger, Howard, and wipe it in that white paint, and put the paint on with your finger." So I did that, and it went on so much smoother with my finger than with a brush. And on the end of that finger where the paint was, there were two eyes, a nose, and a mouth. It seemed as if that face spoke to me. A divine feeling came over me, and it felt as if the face was saying, "Howard, paint sacred art." And I said back, "I can't paint sacred art, Lord.

Professionals can, but not me. I don't know how to." Then I felt the question forming in me—How do you know you can't? Since then I have created over forty thousand works of sacred art. Through my art, I get a lot of the words of Jesus out there for people to see.

✸

Inspiration and revelation turn us into passionate people. We become clear-sighted and productive, and we want the world to know, or the world just seems to know, that in our work and in our lives there has been a change. We have been guided toward a path that we had not before been on. We have responded to the voice, the breath, the face on our hand, the rumbling in our heart.

In Scripture we read that Jesus' disciples "were all filled with the Holy Spirit and spoke the word of God boldly" (Acts 4:31—NIV). The disciples had become clear-sighted and productive about sharing the teachings of Christ. They had become bold in revealing the Spirit of God because His Spirit was within them. There is a tendency in all of us to share what is within us. When we are filled with anger, we are bold in our anger. When we are filled with love, we are bold in our love.

We all know, of course, that it is not our circumstances that fill us. What we have, what we do, what we own, and how things go can be taken away in an instant. Even the best of circumstances can leave us bored and empty and still wanting more. At the age of fifty, Tolstoy stopped writing novels in the midst of a successful career because he felt that sense of emptiness. Against his intellect, and despite the fact that he had considered himself to have happy life circumstances—health, artistic success, and wealth—he was dissatisfied and restless. He felt that nothing he had had meaning without God. He has been quoted as saying: "Why do I look farther? a voice within me asked. He is there: he, without whom one cannot live. To acknowledge God and to live are one and the same thing. God is what life is."[3]

God is what life is because we are filled with his breath, and to breathe is to be alive. For Tolstoy, who turned away from an abundant life, God was what made life abundant.

This is also true of the musician Christopher Parkening. Parkening is one of the world's preeminent classical guitar virtuosos. In 1977, Parkening had reached such a high level of financial success that he was able to retire from performing and recording at the age of thirty. Like Tolstoy, he had everything he had thought he ever wanted, but he still felt empty. In 1982, Parkening returned to his music career by recording *Simple Gifts,* which included spirituals, hymns, and traditional sacred pieces from the classical repertoire. In the liner notes to *Simple Gifts,* Parkening wrote, "I feel privileged to offer these sacred works to you and to share in music the joy and hope of the Christian life. It is my hope that in some small way this album may be my 'simple gift' to honor and glorify my Lord and Savior, Jesus Christ."[4]

The following is Parkening's story.

CHRISTOPHER PARKENING

I started guitar at the age of eleven with the inspiration of a cousin of mine who, at the time, was staff guitarist at MGM Studios. When I asked him about studying the guitar, he suggested two things to me. He said, "First, start with classical guitar and get a good foundation in guitar technique." And then he said, "Get the records of Andrés Segovia. He's the greatest guitarist in the world." So I went out and bought Segovia's records, started classical guitar, loved it, and stayed with it. In 1964, after I studied for about four years, I received a scholarship to Segovia's first United States Master Class at the University of California at Berkeley. I was the youngest of nine performing students to attend that class. At the age of nineteen, I was fortunate to be able to sign a contract with Capitol Records—Angel Records, same company—for a series of six recordings. The following year, I signed with Columbia Artists Management and started a concert career. I was playing over ninety concerts a year, all over the United States, Canada, Europe, Asia. Concurrent with that, I was asked to start a guitar department at the University of Southern California while I was still attending school. So everything made for a very busy life growing up, and somewhat of a busy, fast-paced career.

Through my twenties, I was playing these ninety concerts a year, really with a goal in mind. My father had retired at the age of forty-seven. I had gotten some advice from some people who said if I could make a lot of money with the guitar, I could retire at an early age and enjoy the good life. And so I set my goal on retiring at the age of thirty.

Also, I should say that growing up, even before the guitar, I had a great love of the mountains and the out-of-doors, but in particular fly-fishing for trout. My folks would take my sister and me up to a ranch in the High Sierras of Northern California, and there I learned the art of dry fly-fishing, and that's when I was the happiest. So my goal in life was to some day own my own ranch and trout stream, and be able to retire at an early age.

I found a ranch with a beautiful trout stream in the southwest part of the state of Montana, and so I moved up there at about the age of thirty. I had everything that I ever thought would make me happy. I made a call to Columbia Artists Management in New York, and a similar call to Capitol Records, and said, "Thank you. It's been nice, but I found my life's dream, and I don't desire to tour or record anymore." I also called USC and said I was not going to be able to teach at the music department there anymore. I didn't play the guitar professionally for the next four years. I had everything that I ever thought would have made me happy, and yet I still felt empty inside, and unfulfilled. I thought, You mean this is what I spent all that time in hotel rooms for? And airplane flights and grueling schedules? I did all of that work just so I could have this? It was not what I thought it would be.

I went to California to visit some friends and family, and a neighbor happened to lean over a backyard fence and invite me to a Bible-teaching church, which happened to be Grace Community Church. Pastor John MacArthur preached a sermon which he titled "Examine yourselves, whether you be in the faith," from Matthew 7, where Jesus said, "Not everyone that saith unto me, Lord, Lord, shall enter into the kingdom of heaven; but he that doeth the will of my Father which is in heaven. Many will say to me in that day, Lord, Lord, have we not . . . in thy name done many wonderful works? And then will I profess unto them, I never knew you: depart from me" (21–23).

And when he spoke those words from the Bible, my whole life flashed in front of me. I thought, I'm not a Christian! I would stand before Christ, and He would say to me, "You never cared about the things of Christ. You never cared about being obedient to my commands. You never cared about glorifying me with your life or your music. All you ever cared about was your ranches and your trout streams." And He would say to me, "Depart from me, I never knew you. I never had any intimate relationship with you."

It was at that point that I really believed I wasn't a Christian. I mean, I believed some facts about Christ. I believed that He was the Son of God, and that He died on a cross for the sins of the world. And I believed that He rose again the third day. But I never really wanted a Lord in my life. Maybe I wanted a Savior to save me from hell, but I never wanted a Lord in my life that I should follow and trust, and be obedient to. I have come to realize, as I read throughout Scripture, that you really can't separate the Saviorhood from the Lordship of Christ. He is both Savior and Lord. That night I went home, broken over my sins, and the emptiness of my life, the wasted opportunities with the guitar, and playing the instrument for the wrong motives. I asked Christ to come into my life. And I remember saying, "Whatever you want me to do, Lord, I'll do it."

From that moment on, I had a great hunger for the Word of God, for what Scripture said. I was reading through the Bible one day, and I came across a passage in 1 Corinthians which said, "Whatever you do, do all for the glory of God" (10:31—NASB), and I realized there were only two things that I knew how to do. One was to fly-fish for trout, and the other was to play the guitar. The latter seemed the best option to pursue. So I made a call to Columbia Artists Management, and to Capitol Records, and said, "Guess what? I want to start playing the guitar again, but this time for a different purpose." That purpose would be to honor and glorify my Lord and Savior, Jesus Christ. That was the purpose for me.

I had always been inspired, even growing up, by the music of Bach. But even more so when I read what he said about music: "The aim and final reason of all music is none else but the glory of God." After many of his compositions, he wrote the initials S.D.G., Latin for *Soli Deo Gloria*—"To God alone, the glory." I thought if Bach could use his great ability and talent for that purpose, that would be the least that I could do with whatever ability or talent God had given me.

So I went back on the road again for a different purpose. I essentially threw away a valuable career, and by God's grace He has given that back to me. I realize honestly that whatever talent or ability any of us has been given, it has been given to us by God, and we're responsible to be good stewards of that talent. You know, the interesting thing to me is that so many people are working toward a retirement when they will be "happy," and I was able to experience the fulfillment of a dream at thirty, and I found out it wasn't what I thought it was going to be. I think about the myriad of people who are working toward this time in their lives when they will retire, when they will finally be happy and fulfilled, but if you don't have Christ in your life it is bound to be emptiness. Knowing this has given me a deep-down joy and fulfillment and peace, and a purpose for living that I never had before.

⊞

In most every cliché there is an element of falseness and truth. We can't select a birthday card without reading a quip like "Today is the first day of *what's left* of your life," and we are not spared people around us using standard clichés like "The grass is always greener on the other side." Though it is true that we are living what is left of our lives, and that we want greener grass than we have, *each* day marks what is left of our lives, and we all know that the grass we want is not always greener.

Whether that grass is a new job, a new house, a marriage, success, or to retire at the age of thirty, the thrill of having these things may not come or not last. We are a culture that wants what we want, and then tires of it fast. We are often like children on their birthdays opening presents. In a frenzy, they unwrap gifts they had asked for—that they *had* to have—and become overexcited and, eventually, over-tired, and then sometimes bored after playing for ten minutes.

The thrill does not last because what we want does not last. Toys come and go. Jobs, houses, marriages, and success come and go as well. When God reveals Himself, when He inspires us, it is to say, *I will last, my Spirit will last; when my Spirit is within you what you do will be lasting.*

God reveals Himself and inspires us in different ways. During our conversation with Dr. Rama Coomaraswamy, a thoracic and cardiovascular surgeon, psychiatrist, and Mother Teresa's first volunteer, he said, "There are two kinds of revelations. There is the formal revelation, which is preserved by the church, and then there are private revelations. The distinction is a theological one, between those revelations which are provided by either tradition or Scripture, and by what

God may manifest to someone privately. We're not obliged as Catholics to accept a private revelation as truth. But we can. However, as a Catholic I can't reject the existence of the Trinity because that's not a private revelation, it is a part of the body of revealed faith."

In the stories we have read so far about revelation—Baylor's, Finster's, and Parkening's—there has been a combination of private revelation and revelation provided by Scripture. God revealed to each of them something about their lives and about His Spirit through a personal awakening, and also through His Word. Those of faith believe that what is in Scripture and in other religious texts are the truths that are revealed by God, on which people base their faith.

In Christianity there is a set of givens on which people base their faith. Christopher Parkening referred to those givens or truths as "facts" in relation to Christ: "I believed that He was the Son of God, and He died on a cross for the sins of the world. And I believed that He rose again the third day." For Christians, this is indisputable. All religions have their set of facts that, for them, are indisputable. These events belong to a past that cannot be changed, and it is believed that these events have been divinely revealed. They are the foundation.

To live one's life in honor of these events, as Baylor, Finster, and Parkening have come to do, means that everything they now do, they do for the purpose of glorifying God. This is what their revelations have moved them to do. They no longer see their work and their faith as separate.

This is also true of professional basketball player Hakeem Olajuwon. Olajuwon was born in Lagos, Nigeria, on the west coast of Africa, and grew up in a Muslim family. As a six-foot-eight-inch teenager, Hakeem excelled as a soccer player. Because of his height, he was advised to try basketball, and he mastered the sport in just a few years. Olajuwon grew to his present height of six feet eleven inches, and went on to become one of the National Basketball Association's premier players. He led the Houston Rockets to consecutive NBA championships in 1994 and 1995.

As a child, Olajuwon felt deeply about his religion, and would often stop by a mosque on the way to school and recite passages from the Qur'an with others. But he eventually drifted away from his religion and concentrated instead on sports. At the age of twenty-five, when he was already recognized as one of the top players in the NBA, Olajuwon was invited to a local mosque, in Houston, for Friday prayers. Up until that time, he had felt that there was something missing in his life, though he could not define what it was. That night, the presence of God was so strong for him that, while worshiping, he had a vivid recollection of the faith he had as a child. He felt that God was guiding him back to this faith. From that moment, he made a commitment to devoting substantial time to study, to prayer, and to observing Islamic ritual. Before this experience, Olajuwon felt that he had been living his life according to his own understanding, and not in alignment with God's will. Now he no longer sees anything that he does, including basketball, as separate from his religion.

HAKEEM OLAJUWON

I now look at my career in a totally different way than when I first came into the National Basketball Association. Back then it was just competition. Now I look at basketball as part of my religion. It's not separate. The way I play basketball, the way I deal with my coworkers, with my coaches, with all the people around me is all part of my faith. Whether you're getting paid a lot or a little, you have to perform the same way, because your duty is not to the company that you work for. Your duty is to God. Intention is very important when your goal is clear. And the beauty of it is, when you do an excellent job at work with the right intention, which is to please God, you will be rewarded apart from the reward you get from your work. You will be rewarded by God. You cannot get this kind of a reward from materialism or accomplishment. That's a different kind of satisfaction. It's not even close to the gratification you get from spiritual inspiration and accomplishment.

People ask me all the time, "After all these years, how can you be inspired and motivated? What is challenging for you?" The answer is that my intention is always to please God.

Though Olajuwon continues to be inspired and motivated in his work, as do Baylor, Finster, and Parkening, he studies what Muslims believe to be the revealed Word of God, a different sacred text than the Christian Bible. Clearly the Bible and the Qur'an are fundamentally different in their revealed faith. Divine incarnation and atonement, which are at the heart of Christian faith, are foreign to Muslim thought. Muslims do not believe in a Savior who died for our sins, and Christians do not believe, as Muslims do, that no soul can bear the sins of another.

And yet, we see that people of different religions have been inspired and empowered by the Spirit of God. There are conflicting views in each tradition as to what is the "true" revelation of God. In so many cases, though the beliefs may be different, the result of inspiration is the same.

We have all seen those before-and-after weight-loss ads on television that show us those dark photographs of the overweight person next to the same bright, glowing person who now looks thin and lively and proud. There are many competing products and many different ads all showing the same result. Each person will swear by the product that has brought him or her that result, but the outsider will note the result before using the product.

The point is not that weight-loss products are comparable to religious faith. It is that, when it comes to inspiration and revelation, people of competing faiths often see the same result. Each tradition has its own understanding of the nature and purpose of God. To seek this understanding is to seek God, and He will often lead us to the path where we can find Him.

Revelation is one of the ways by which we find that path, and inspiration is what keeps us on it. As we have seen from the stories in this chapter, once God reveals Himself to us, if we choose to live according to His will for our lives, the way we see things and who we are will change. There is a before and after in our understanding of the divine, and in our actions in response to this understanding.

After a grueling bout with pancreatic cancer, a very well-respected Lutheran minister and professor of church history died. His daughter, Kari Lee Hart, a self-described "occasional churchgoer," said that her faith took shape as she watched her father pass away. At the moment that he died, Hart, for the first time in her life, felt the presence of God's Spirit. She sensed clearly that her father had been taken by God.

KARI LEE HART

My father spent a hellish night the last night he was alive. He had been in intense pain—even more so than the intense pain he had lived with on and off for two years. I believe his illness tested his faith. He was a man of great faith, and yet he was angry. He went through a *"why me"* phase for a long time, but I know the theologian in him knew that his questions would only make his faith stronger. It is inevitable that at some point, something will test your faith in God. God doesn't test you. Life does.

I had never been with anyone who died. I was terrified by the whole aspect of dying. My father died at home, and around his death bed were my mother, my sister, our pastor, and the woman who had helped deliver my two children. It was quiet except for the sound of the machine with the morphine, and my father's breathing. For about an hour we prayed. Our pastor read a couple of the Psalms. Soon my father's breathing began to slip, then stop, and all we heard was the noise from the machine. I looked up at the woman who had helped deliver my children, and she nodded at me as if to say, This is it. As I watched my father die, for the first time in my life I actually saw what I never before could imagine—his body had stopped, who he was was gone, and I saw clearly that he had been taken, that someone had taken him. I was not of great faith at that time, in fact I felt distant from God, and angry, and yet the sense I had of my father being taken is unshakable. One minute he was here, and the next minute I'm looking out the window, hearing the birds sing, and realizing that he was far beyond that, that he had been taken by God, by Jesus, but that he had not ceased to exist. In birth you exist in the womb, then you leave there and begin to exist in this world. When we leave this world, we will begin to exist somewhere else.

The other day I read Frederick Buechner's *The Magnificent Defeat.* I go back to the day of my father's death, and I'm starting to connect what happened to something that Buechner said:

> *To be a saint is to live not with the hands clenched to grasp, to strike, to hold tight to a life that is always slipping away the more tightly we hold it; but it is to live with the hands stretched out both to give and to receive with gladness. To be a saint is to work and weep for the broken and suffering of the world, but it is also to be strangely light of heart in the knowledge that there is something greater than the world that mends and renews. Maybe more than anything else, to be a saint is to know joy. Not happiness that comes*

and goes with the moments that occasion it, but joy that is always there like an underground spring no matter how dark and terrible the night. [5]

And then I think of Dad's breath slowing, stopping, the nod that said, This is it. And at that exact moment, when Jesus took my father, the tightness left and God's Spirit came into me and filled me. I went from hands clenched tightly to hands and heart stretched out. And I was, strangely, light of heart.

The image I have had of my father's death is of melodies that finally came together and made a beautiful song. For me, it was like a jigsaw puzzle. All those pieces—his illness and his pain—all over the table and making no sense. Just a big jumble of pieces. And his dying was the beginning of those pieces starting to come together and making sense. I literally had an awakening. At one point I did not see God's love, His presence, and after my father died, I did. I was vulnerable, open, raw, in total pain, and maybe there was an opening in my soul that made me receptive, and let this vision in. They say faith suffuses you with life. Well, for me it did.

I started reading, reflecting on it, going to church, and all of a sudden these words started to make sense, and I started to take them to heart. I had known the Lutheran service word for word, but it had meant nothing before. All of a sudden I was saying these words, understanding them, and being inspired by them. I had seen God at work—His comfort, His love. At my most vulnerable point, I was shown that there is an end to the suffering, there is an end to pain. There is no end to God's love.

Just as the revelation that Hakeem Olajuwon received inspired him to increase his commitment to prayer, and to observing religious rituals, the revelation that Hart received inspired her to do the same. She began to pray and to attend church regularly, and she is currently pursuing a master's degree of Divinity in a Lutheran seminary, the same seminary where her father had taught.

To watch someone die, and to see a beginning as opposed to just an ending, is to see death as a passage from here to beyond here, in the way that birth is a passage from not being in this world to beginning one's life in this world.

Just before my grandmother died of emphysema, she lay on her hospital bed weaving in and out of consciousness. She had been out of consciousness for quite a while, and then abruptly opened her eyes and announced, "I'm going now." She knew she was going and, within an hour, she went. My grandmother did not believe in God, and I always wanted to know what it was she saw and heard in the darkness of her sleep. What stirred me was the word *now*—I am going *now*—that she knew that at this specific moment, her body was about to stop. And yet despite this, she was in motion. She was going.

I have wondered if what she saw, at the end, was what Hart saw—the human spirit, in the care of God's Spirit, being taken to somewhere beyond here. For my grandmother to have seen this would account for the peace she seemed to have had just before she died. For Hart to have seen this would explain why that aspect of her father's death would have suffused her with life.

The breath of God, the life-giving Spirit of God, is present when we are in motion. We tend to think of death as the opposite of motion. We see it as final, as the ending of a relationship and a life. To think of someone's spirit being taken, of passing from here to somewhere else accompanied by the life-giving breath of God, is to think of God as always being beside us; it is to think of our spirits as always being beside God. Not to believe this and then to see it as someone dies would be a turning point in one's faith. Though Hart certainly cannot prove or adequately explain what she saw when she sensed that her father's spirit was being taken, what is significant is that whatever it was she saw, which could have left her bitter and tight, opened her spirit rather than closed it.

No one can adequately explain faith or inspiration. Words do not fully convey the prompting inside us, or our sense that something that cannot be proven is true. It is important to distinguish between facts and truth. Facts are things that we can prove and see, aspects of science, mathematics, certain events in our lives. It is a fact that you painted a portrait of a man, that you gave birth to a girl, that you held your father's hand as he was dying. But truth is what we *know,* not necessarily what can be physically seen—that you were inspired when you painted, that this is who you love, or who you do not love, that something stirred you as you were praying.

When we met with Rabbi Alexander Schindler, he said, "I think that one of the hindrances to the modern mind in accepting the idea of God is the fact that people insist that the only thing which is real is that which can be perceived by the physical senses. But there is an invisible world, and that world is just as real as the world that is seen. Ideas are real and have the power to transform our lives, but they are certainly invisible. Ideals are imperceptible, yet they can also transform lives. Music and art are mysteries. One wonders how inspiration can come through vessels that are human and imperfect."

Schindler felt led to become a rabbi after he entered college as an engineering student. At the outbreak of World War II, he left college to enlist as an army volunteer, where he served as a forward observer for mountain artillery. After the defeat of the German army, Schindler was stationed with the Allied troops on the Yugoslavian border. Since there was no longer an active war, Schindler was allowed to drive north into Germany to investigate the whereabouts of his family. In Munich, and then in Dachau, he found that thirty-five members of his family had been killed, including his aunts, nephews and nieces, and his grandparents. This experience had a profound effect on Schindler. When he returned to college in the United States, he immediately switched from the engineering department to the social studies department. He immersed himself in Jewish studies with the hope of finding some understanding of the Holocaust. He was eventually ordained as a rabbi in 1953, and served as president of the Union of American Hebrew Congregations from 1973 until 1996, when he retired at the age of seventy. Under his leadership, the congregational body of Reform Judaism has become the fastest-growing denomination of Judaism in North America, with 1.5 million members throughout the United States and Canada.

Learning that thirty-five members of his family were killed in the Holocaust is not solely what led Schindler to become a rabbi. It was also something inside his spirit that he could not see, that guided and empowered him to change the focus of his life.

Rabbi Schindler went on to say: "It is interesting that science, which we tend to accept with greater ease than we accept God, very often accepts certain things that are not necessarily seen. For instance, there is something called a cloud chamber, which allows the physicist to trace subatomic particles that are too small to be seen by the eye, which might never be seen, but are evidenced only through its traces. Similarly, I find God through the traces that He leaves in the world. In love that evokes willing sacrifices from us, in the beauty of life, I find traces of God, and I accept them, just as the physicist accepts the existence of particles that simply cannot be seen."

When the renowned scientist Carl Sagan passed away in 1996, his friend the Reverend Joan Brown Campbell, general secretary of the National Council of Churches, made the following comment during the eulogy: "He would say to me, 'You are so smart, why do you believe in God?' And I would say, 'You are so smart, why don't you believe in God?' "[6]

This wry observation speaks volumes about the often polarized relationship that has existed between religion and modern science. Ironically, the pioneers of modern science—Newton, Galileo, Descartes, and Kepler—could all be regarded as religious men, in the sense that they viewed science as man's ability to describe, and to learn from, God's work. However, a major shift away from any theological aspects of scientific thought occurred in the beginning of the nineteenth century, when Pierre-Simon Laplace and other French mathematicians proposed a mechanistic view of the universe, in which a belief in God was unnecessary. This theory attempted to show that the science of mechanics provided a complete view of nature without a religious component. Though mathematics still remains the best language for describing physical properties, recent experiments and research have increasingly supported the belief that the universe is divinely designed.

The respected particle physicist John Polkinghorne spoke about the strained relationship between science and theology. Polkinghorne, a former Cambridge professor of mathematical physics, is the author of six books that explore various aspects of science and religion. Polkinghorne was ordained as a priest in the Anglican Church in 1982. From 1989 to 1996 he was president of Queens College, Cambridge. The interview with Polkinghorne took place while he spent two months at the General Theological Seminary in New York City.

JOHN POLKINGHORNE

As a religious believer, and a physicist, it seems to me that the mind of God can be discerned in the beautiful structure of the world. Many of my colleagues, of course, wouldn't choose to interpret it that way. Certainly twentieth-century physics already has seen the death of a merely mechanical view of the world, because of quantum theory and also because of chaos theory. There is a great deal of intrinsic unpredictability, which I think is best interpreted as intrinsic flexibility, built into the system of the world. And moreover, we've learned that you can't understand the physical world simply by taking things apart and looking at the bits and pieces of which they're made. There is something in quantum theory which is called the EPR effect (Einstein, Podolsky, Rosen), and this EPR effect says that once two quantum entities, say a couple of electrons or something like that, have interacted with each other, they retain a power to influence each other, however far they separate. So modern science is seeing that there are interconnections between things in the world. The point is you still learn things by taking things apart, but you can't learn everything by doing so.

I worked in the physics of elementary particles. And I actually lived through a very interesting phase in that subject, when one saw, for the first time, a new pattern of structure in the world that was very beautiful, and concise, and that could be expressed in mathematics. All of us who were a part of this enterprise were left with a sense of wonder at the beautiful structure of the world. It seemed to me that it was the mind of God that was being discerned.

Another individual whom we spoke with regarding the issue of religion and science was Dr. Jeffrey B. Satinover. Dr. Satinover is a practicing psychiatrist who holds degrees from the Massachusetts Institute of Technology and the Harvard Graduate School of Education. He was subsequently invited by Harvard to deliver the prestigious William James Lectures in Psychology and Religion. Dr. Satinover lectures widely on topics ranging from brain neurophysiology to the breakdown of modern society.

When Satinover was very young, he was attracted to mystery. "Throughout my childhood," he told us, "physics was a great love, and interest, and goal of mine. But without knowing it, I was also fearful that I wasn't going to live up to my own expectations, and so I did not pursue it." As an adult, in the context of healing prayer, Satinover, who is Jewish, felt that his inhibitions to pursue physics had been lifted. Currently studying toward a doctorate in physics at Yale, Satinover believes that "the discoveries that are at the heart of physics will make people aware of the fact—not just aware, it will make it second nature to them the way materialism is second nature now—that the entire physical universe is permeated at every level with a mystery that is fundamentally theological in nature."

Satinover cites the experiments conducted under the direction of the physicist Alain Aspect, at the University of Paris-South, as being instrumental in supporting a belief in the active presence of God in the cosmos. Aspect's experiments, published in 1982, resulted in experimental confirmation that there is something at work in the universe that influences all physical events, yet which lies outside the domain of modern scientific knowledge.

JEFFREY B. SATINOVER, M.D.

The worldview that modern science has depended on, for the most part, is this: if you have 100 percent knowledge of an initial condition, then all subsequent conditions are known as well. If this were true, there would be no such thing as free will, whether human or divine. God himself would be a merely passive observer who not only doesn't but *couldn't* have an effect on the world. And human beings couldn't have an effect either, because if all physical events are, in effect, laid out ahead of time, like a complex play in billiards, then nothing one does can alter the outcome. It's all completely determined. This is the fundamental premise of the modern worldview. However, it turns out, and what modern physics has now demon-

LEONTYNE PRICE,
Opera Singer. JACK MITCHELL

ANDRE DUBUS,
Author. MARION ETTLINGER

J. CARTER BROWN, *Director Emeritus of the National Gallery of Art, Washington, DC.* LAURA ALLEN NOEL

DOC WATSON, *Musician.* KENNETH S. LEWIS

WYNTON MARSALIS, *Musician.* FRANK STEWART

DR. LORI WIENER, *Coordinator of the Pediatric HIV Psychosocial Support Program at the National Cancer Institute.* BILL LEBOVICH

DESMOND TUTU,
Archbishop of South Africa.

DAVID W. CHECKETTS,
*President and CEO of Madison Square
Garden, New York City.* NAT BUTLER

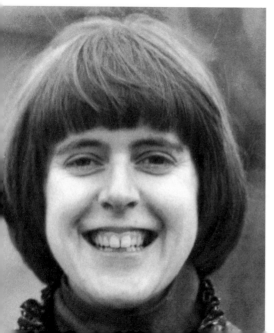

KATHLEEN NORRIS,
Author. DAVID DWYER

ANG LEE, *Filmmaker.*

KENNETH S. LEWIS

RABBI ALEXANDER
M. SCHINDLER, *President of the
Union of American Hebrew Congregations,
1973–1996.* GEORGE KALINSKY

DR. LORRAINE HALE, *Co-founder and President of Hale House,
New York City.* SHAHAR AZRAN

DR. MICHAEL E. DeBAKEY, M.D., *Chancellor Emeritus, Baylor University, and Director of the DeBakey Heart Center.*

DIANA ECK, *Professor of Comparative Religion and Indian Studies at Harvard University.* LILLIAN KEMP

BENJAMIN HIRSCH,
Architect. JANE LEAVEY

PANDURANG SHASTRI
ATHAVALE, *Philosopher.*

HAKEEM OLAJUWON, *Athlete.* BARRY GOSSAGE / NBA PHOTOS

MADELEINE
L'ENGLE, *Author.*

KENNETH S. LEWIS

VISHWA MOHAN
BHATT, *Musician.*

SALIL V. BHATT

strated is, that's not true. That actually, at the most fundamental level, all of the most important physical processes are, in part, determined by "factors" that have no detectable presence in the physical world. A range of possible outcomes are determined mechanically, but untold numbers of decisions are being made by "something" that from among these possibilities selects every actual outcome. And furthermore, each time a decision is made, all other probabilities are instantaneously adjusted and altered so as to keep the whole system within certain bounds. This is not a philosophical concept. This is a description of what has been shown, to the shock and horror of many scientists, in actual physical experiments. The only way to talk about it metaphorically is that there's "something" that is not part of the physical universe, which sits outside it, and simultaneously orchestrates all events throughout the entire universe, according to principles that we can't know. My own particular angle on this is that if there is this effect that is sustaining the universe in an ongoing way, causing results, but it itself has no prior cause, well, that is one of the oldest definitions of God.

Those who pursue science and those who pursue God share a common goal. They both want to discover what is true. The study of science reveals and helps us to better appreciate the beauty and mystery of the universe. Discoveries that come through physics can tell us about the physical world, and can disclose, as Satinover put it, that something "is sustaining the universe in an ongoing way."

The breath of God is sustaining the universe in an ongoing way. It can lead people, in all fields and circumstances, to the place where God's Spirit can be revealed.

CREATIVITY

God is constantly creating, in us, through us,
and with us, and to co-create with God
is our human calling.[1]

MADELEINE L'ENGLE,
Walking on Water:
Reflections on Faith and Art

MARK DOTY

When I was growing up in Tennessee, my grandmother and I used to sing hymns on the porch swing on summer nights, and the poetry of those songs, and the poetry of the Bible stories that I heard from her and that I heard in Sunday school, were essential to me. It wasn't their specific content, or the way those religious images were viewed that were particularly influential for me. But what was and remains influential is the power of the imagery itself, the poetry of the imagery and its suggestion that meaning lies behind the surface of ordinary things, that there is more to the world than you can see.

A lot of poets, and myself among them, talk about their poems in a sort of mystical way, which suggests that the poem is more something we find than something we make. As if it already existed out there somewhere and it came to us. There is a deeper part of the self speaking, and I think that deeper part of the self is where we experience our connection to other lives or to a life that is larger than ours. I need to move into a state of quiet so that I can experience that connection, and so that I can be receptive to inspiration.

The beginning of something that I write is like—if you could see it, it would be this luminous seed, this beautiful, shiny seed, and when I first apprehend it or know it's there, I don't know what kind of plant it is going to be, but with this seed I am given this little knot of potentiality that is full of life and energy, and it is going to be something really specific if I pay attention to it. And pretty soon I might get an image that feels charged and interesting and alive. One image collects another and another and pretty soon something has tumbled out and I always feel as if I don't know where this comes from. All I know is that it comes from somewhere beneath the surface of things, and I think one way we could define God would be that absence or that not-being out of which things come.

All creative vision involves looking beyond and beneath the surface of things. There is more to the world than what meets the eye, the heart, or the mind. This is the mystery of creation. Inspiration is often first thought of in relation to creativity, for creativity relies on vision, and inspiration is what guides our vision. In every act of creation, there is a movement from not seeing, or from partly seeing, to revelation.

The mystery of inspiration is at the heart of the artist's vision. Inspiration is also at the heart of our vision when we seek to see God. Not all creative people seek God, or even believe in God, and not all believers would call themselves creative. But those who create and those who seek God both look beyond the surface of the world and leave themselves open to inspiration. Words that are written in poetry and words said in prayer often come forth without understanding. They seem to "tumble out," as Doty said. To allow them to tumble out, not quite knowing where they are tumbling from, is an act of faith. In this sense, the person who prays and the poet are vessels. Something beyond them passes through them. Something inspires them to speak and to write.

The image of being a vessel is a common image among those who are inspired. Vessels are what the authors of Scripture are known to have been. They were guided and filled with the Spirit of God, with an outpouring of His breath. God the Spirit breathed on them, inspired them to speak and write, and these individuals, who had their own personalities—talents, quirks, and failings—became vessels that were filled with divine inspiration. But what does this say about inspiration? If God guides what people create, who is the creator?

The composer Igor Stravinsky had been known to answer the question this way: when speaking about the source of his compositions, he said, "Only God can create. I make music from music."[2]

If the world—if every living, breathing thing in the world—is brought to life with the breath of God, then one could say that every person in the world creates in relation to the Creator. God created man in His image, and man, in turn, also creates. To believe that inspiration is divine action, and that we are vessels for this divine action, does not mean that we are passive and uninvolved. When Doty says that "the poem is more something we find than something we make," the point is that it is still the poet's job to make something out of what he finds. To create, just as to pray, involves listening, and both involve action. We accomplish nothing unless we put into action what we have listened to, until we pursue what we have heard.

During our conversation with filmmaker Ang Lee, who has directed, among other films, *The Ice Storm, Sense and Sensibility,* and *The Wedding Banquet,* he expressed feelings similar to what Doty expressed. Lee believes that the images and ideas that come to him are not a product of his will, but that he makes something from what already exists, from what is sent to him, from what he finds. He has found that his perspective has been influenced by Buddhist philosophy, which teaches that through a path of moral practice and meditation that aims to calm the mind, one can rest in a state of nothingness, without the illusion produced by desire. The belief is that by not striving, one will eventually be led to peace, and to enlightenment.

ANG LEE

I believe that all we create is sent from somewhere. It is as if our ideas already exist, and pass through us in order to be seen. What is up in the air comes down and comes through you. If a movie works, it has a life of its own. The director's job is to find the life of the movie, and when it comes alive with the audiences, it is out of the director's hands. Once the movie goes to the theater, I hardly feel anything, even watching it. It has used me, and then it is gone.

All my life, when things have happened that have worked out successfully, it has been because of what has come to me, not from what I have willed. However, in my thirties, I was not having success. I didn't get work for six years. This was very tough to go through as a filmmaker, a struggling artist. Many scripts and projects did not work out for me. I walked around a lot every day. It was a very difficult time. At night it was very hard to fall asleep. I would look at the stars, and feel how big the universe is, and how small we are. Universal laws, natural laws, do exist, and are beyond human understanding. Seeing how meaningless existence can be sort of lightened up my burden, and helped me pass through these years.

During this time, I began to read books about Buddhism, which were very enlightening. I started meditating and doing tai chi, which helped me calm down. I feel totally religious, but not in a formal way. I think balance is the key, not going to any extreme. This is very Chinese. As a human being, I would like to be humble, to try to keep a balance, and to observe what is going on beyond this life. I believe that the best ideas and inspiration come from something beyond us, from something that is above us, rotating. When I try to force my ideas to fit an agenda, it never works.

※

When inspiration comes, it does not come by will. We are led and we receive. We know that something is being sent to us, but the mystery involves the sender.

In Buddhism, unlike other religions, there is hardly any mention of God. During our conversation, Lee made a point of saying that "The real orthodox Buddhism is not about worshiping something, it is about the principle of nothingness." Inspiration for Lee comes from something he cannot name, except to say that it is "something that is above us, rotating." For those who create, and for those of faith, it is difficult to convey, or to truly define, what is rotating above us, guiding us, redefining our vision. And yet we are as quick to try to define it as we are to deny it. We have all been witness to, or have heard about, heated conversations between believers and nonbelievers, or between believers and other believers who believe in a different way. The declarations of who God is, or who God is not, fly back and forth.

A man I know once said to another man, "You talk about God as if you know him, as if you could tell me the color of his eyes. Why do people keep creating something to worship? I make it a point not to believe in anything that always has the upper hand."

"Then how do you explain the world?" the other man said. "How come you're here?"

"Because it happened. Things just happen."

"Well, maybe 'things just happen' is another name for God."

Along these lines, we might say that "things just happen" is another name for inspiration. We often don't know what to call the stirrings inside us that guide and empower us to create, and those stirrings cannot be adequately conveyed or described to others in the way that they are felt and reflected in the work. Yet, if we believe that there is something beyond our human capacities of imagination and sight, then we can call creative inspiration a result of our being in the presence of the divine.

The way we express our imagination and vision is shaped by who we are. During our conversation, Ang Lee said, "I heard an American director say, 'Oh, all Chinese filmmakers are good with metaphor. When was the last time we American filmmakers used metaphor? How dare we say that Americans are the best filmmakers?' My response should have been, What do *you* need metaphor for? Americans don't need metaphor. I grew up using metaphor because there was a lot of oppression and prohibition in my society, so I have tried to find a way to zigzag into what I want to express."

This statement does not mean that the way we express ourselves as artists is entirely defined by our history, but, to a good degree, our vision is shaped by the way we have come to see the world. Though it is true that at any point in time inspiration can redefine our vision, we are often working against certain givens. This subject was also addressed during our conversation with Andre Dubus.

ANDRE DUBUS

I'm often asked, "Are you a Catholic writer?" And I say, "Yes, because I only see the world as a Catholic." If I were a practicing Jew, I would see the world as a practicing Jew. If I were a Lutheran, I would see the world as a Lutheran. If I were a Muslim, I would see the world as a Muslim. But I'm Catholic, so whether my characters are Catholic or not, I'm always seeing eternity in my life, I hope, and in my work. I'm always seeing sacraments and forgiveness and variations of sin.

The fact that an artist is religious does not mean that he or she will produce religious art. The Catholic artist does not produce Catholic art any more than a Buddhist artist produces Buddhist art. Art is art, whether or not it has religious themes or whether or not the artist that produced it was religious. It must be looked at as a piece of work that either moves people or does not.

Often the most religious artists will produce work with secular themes, or will use their art to show a different perspective. The author Flannery O'Connor, who was a devout believer and practicing Catholic, often created characters who were fanatical as a result of their religious beliefs. The subject of the work does not have to be pious for it to draw us toward God. We can feel more inspired from reading a masterful story about atheists than we can from reading a poorly written story about saints. We respond first to the mastery reflected in the work. And inspiration is what makes the work masterful.

This is not to say that the nonbeliever cannot produce a work of art, nor does it mean that only believers can be inspired. By grace, inspiration will sometimes stir the most unlikely of spirits. The main difference between the nonbeliever and the artist who seeks God is intention. The believer's purpose in creating the work is often to bring us closer to spiritual matters and, therefore, closer to God. And even if it was not consciously his intention to bring us closer to God, if the work has been inspired, he will.

Thomas Merton wrote in his book *The Ascent to Truth* that the difference between the soul that operates on the human level of inspiration "and of one that is moved on the higher level of the Gifts, by special inspirations of God, is something like the difference between a symphony played by a piano tuner and one played by a genius."[3] His point is that one soul is moved by reason and by human faculties, and may produce work by grace, but only the work that has been divinely inspired can be divine.

The human vision sees only so much. Often when we create, we are led to see something entirely different from what we had first envisioned. We must be willing to abandon our agenda, our preconceived notions about both composition and purpose, in order to serve the work.

This idea of letting go of our agenda is addressed in the following excerpt from our interview with Tobias Wolff. Wolff is the noted author of the memoirs *This Boy's Life* and *In Pharaoh's Army,* and of the short story collections *The Night in Question, Back in the World,* and *In the Garden of the North American Martyrs.*

TOBIAS WOLFF

I remember hearing the pianist Vladimir Ashkenazy give an interview some twenty years ago now, in which he said that when he is playing his best he feels as though he is simply watching, that someone else is doing the playing. I feel that, on occasion. When I sit down to write I usually have a certain idea of what I want to do. But in my best stories I am surprised, and I don't end up following the original idea. Sometimes not only in its details but in its general direction I will completely change things, and who knows where that inspiration comes from? We always want to hang on to the familiar, and creating even a story can be a scary thing. When you have a plan, you hesitate to let go of it because it is a kind of safety, a safety for the mind, for the imagination, to have a road laid out to travel on. But it isn't necessarily and, in fact, is rarely the most interesting or exciting place to go. The courage I feel at times in abandoning the refuge of a preconceived notion for the mystery of one that I do not yet understand and have no idea where it will take me is perhaps how I experience that thing that others are talking about, the sense of being carried along.

I used to think that, as Cocteau said, writers should go to work in the morning like bankers. You sit down and you do it every day. Well, I still think that's true in that you have to be there for it to happen, but in fact what actually goes on when you are sitting down there like a banker, if that is how you want to see it, what actually goes on there is extremely mysterious and humbling because you can't control it, you cannot call it up at will. It is a grace, it is something given to you, it is not something that you have any right to or control over. There is nothing anywhere that says that you are going to be able to complete the idea you have begun. And it is extremely humbling to live that way from day to day.

I think that creative inspiration is a gift of God. But I don't think He's hanging around waiting to give me ideas. We can get silly about this stuff. We can say, "Today I went shopping with God, and he told me what paint to buy." I don't want to trivialize this thing. Inspiration is a gift. We can't count on it. We don't have a right to it. We can't own it. It doesn't always come back. Some people get it once in their lives and do something magnificent with it and never have it again. And because it's such a good thing, so supremely a good thing, I do associate it with God's generosity and with His own creativity.

A few years ago I was at a party where many of the guests were professional dancers. In one of the rooms, most of the furniture had been cleared out so that the guests would be able to dance. I overheard a woman saying that when she choreographed, she waited for God to put her body in different positions. She insisted that in one dance He did this, and then she offered to show a few people from the party this dance. As the woman stepped back, to give herself room, she knocked a vase filled with flowers off a small table. She looked embarrassed, and also curious. "I wonder what He meant by that," she said.

At what point do we take responsibility for the paint we buy, for following through when we create, for the vase we knock off a table? God does intervene in our life, but He does not live our life. He does not make our choices. To choose for us is not to guide us to choose. This would be coercion, not inspiration.

We can take no credit for inspiration, other than for choosing to leave ourselves open to it. This does not mean that it will come when we want it to, or as consistently as we want it to, but by working consistently, just as by praying consistently, we are more likely to receive it.

In this sense, inspiration involves being open and receptive as much as it involves being assertive and active. Our openness is combined with our effort and our skill.

In Scripture, when God inspired Bezaleel, He "filled him with the spirit of God, in wisdom, and in understanding, and in knowledge, and in all manner of workmanship, to devise cunning works, to work in gold, and in silver, and in brass, and in cutting of stones, to set them, and in carving of timber, to work in all manner of workmanship" (Exodus 31:3–5). In the Gospel of Mark, Jesus speaks of David writing Psalm 110 inspired "by the Holy Ghost" (12:36).

Our talents, no matter how large or small, are gifts, and it is our responsibility to use our gifts. Writers must write, musicians are compelled to play whether they feel inspired or not. We cannot count on inspiration to precede the work. More often than not it comes *during* the work.

During our interview with the Hindu musician Vishwa Mohan Bhatt, he said, "Inspiration most often comes to me when I am concentrating deeply on my music." Bhatt believes that as he plays music he receives inspiration from God, and from the Goddess Saraswati (goddess of music and knowledge). The Hindu tradition is based on both monotheist and polytheist beliefs—there is one ultimate God, though this supreme being has many attributes, or deities, that can be worshiped by name. Typically, a Hindu will have a single chosen deity that he or she has selected for special devotion.

Bhatt, who resides in Jaipur, India, has gained international recognition for his performances of Indian classical music on a nineteen-string instrument called the *mohan veena*. Though not all Indian classical music is religious, or devotional, there are many compositions, traditionally referred to as ragas, which are played, or sung, as acts of worship.

VISHWA MOHAN BHATT

During some of my concerts, when I am able to attain a perfect vision of my raga, and when I try to use my imagination to enhance the raga, I have felt that, slowly, I move into somewhat of a trance, and that I lose contact with my audience. I can see the audience, but my mind and body do not realize anybody's presence. I then experience a force which moves me to express my innermost thoughts of devotion through my music, and I become aware that what I am rendering is beyond me. I am able to create combinations of musical notes which I do not know and have never played before. I marvel at what I had played earlier, and feel that it was the divine power that enabled me to bring forth those unheard nuances and intricate passages of music.

Though I have felt this divine power on several occasions, I felt it particularly at work just a couple of days after my eleven-year-old daughter, Surabhi, died. My wife had named her Surabhi. *Sur* means a musical note, and *Surabhi* means the scent of the musical note. She was very different from children of her age. She was very quiet, and used to speak very little, but one could see the light of life on her face. A few days after she died, I was supposed to go to Bangalore to play a concert. This concert was planned about one year in advance. It had been publicized, and the tickets were all sold out, so I was in a fix, whether to go or not. I decided to go, but I didn't know if I would be able to perform. When it was time for me to begin the performance, I was enveloped in grief. With trembling hands, I picked up my instrument and my feet took me to the stage. I remembered Surabhi and began my performance. There was a flow from my heart to my hands. This was God's blessing, that I was able to play, and to move people, and to rise above my grief. When we are inspired by God, our creativity does not stop. Not even death can stop it.

Art is by no means an escape from reality. In serious art we are confronted with reality and truth. We are reminded of the magnificent things in life, and of things that are heart-wrenching, whether we receive the work or create it.

We have all heard the comment that the suffering artist produces the best work. Certainly joyful artists produce great works of art, but it is true that when we suffer, we turn, in passion, to our work, and we often turn to God. To create, in all circumstances, is an act of faith—faith in the work, in ourselves, in something larger than ourselves, faith that in both the magnificent and heart-wrenching things of life, the life-giving spirit of God is there.

The image of this spirit—the breath of God—was incorporated into the creation of *Rings: Five Passions in World Art,* an exhibition that was conceived and directed by J. Carter Brown. Director of the National Gallery of Art in Washington, DC, from 1969 to 1992, and named director emeritus upon his retirement, Brown has been the recipient of many awards, including the National Medal of Arts. He currently serves as chairman of the U.S. Commission of Fine Arts in Washington, DC.

The *Rings* exhibition was shown at Atlanta's High Museum of Art in 1996 as part of the Olympic Arts Festival, and was presented in conjunction with the Centennial Olympic Games. To create *Rings,* Brown took as a model the Olympic symbol of five interlocked rings, and in turn the show was divided into five interlocking themes—

Love, Anguish, Awe, Triumph, and Joy. These themes were illustrated through combinations of works by artists such as Rembrandt, El Greco, van Gogh, Picasso, and Monet, along with paintings and sculptures representing regions and cultures from around the world.

J . CARTER BROWN

My own faith leads me to see God through works of beauty. I may not be as good a church man as I might be, but I do find that I am very responsive to the experience that I have when I attend church. *Rings* has a kind of Christian underlay, and I do make a disclaimer in the catalog that this is a personal view, because it is difficult for one to transcend one's own background. The central section, which I call "Awe," shows a mystical union with the divine. We have a classical music and audio sound track that accompanies the exhibit, and at one point in the section you hear the voice of James Earl Jones reading from a poem called "The Creation," by James Weldon Johnson. It ends with the verse, "This Great God, like a mammy bending over her baby, kneeled down in the dust, toiling over a lump of clay till He shaped it in His own image; then into it He blew the breath of life, and man became a living soul. Amen. Amen."

I mention in the catalog that the word *spirit* and the word *breath* are the same in four languages—Sanskrit *(pragna),* Hebrew *(ruach),* Latin *(spiritus),* and Greek *(pneuma).* And because "The Creation" speaks about breathing a spirit into human form, I have chosen a lot of the images in the "Awe" section to have slightly opened mouths.

The whole idea for *Rings* just came to me. I do not take any credit for it. Only the good Lord knows where this idea, this inspiration, came to me from. *Rings* is about interconnectedness, and what is really the connecting tissue in arts of all times is the emotional and spiritual dimension. I do think that a lot of artists seem to be in touch with mystical forces, and that they draw on some kind of vision and divine inspiration. However, I think there is a romantic idea about the artist who dashes things off in a great blaze of enlightenment. In fact, there probably was such a blaze, at some point in the process, if the artist was inspired, but the realization often takes a tremendous amount of skill, and practice, and hard work.

Enlightenment does not generally arrive in a blaze to those who are not in motion. Though, occasionally, it may seem that we are effortlessly swept away with ideas and inspiration, this inspiration usually was preceded by a good deal of discipline and effort.

The author Madeleine L'Engle addressed this subject during our interview. L'Engle is the author of more than forty books for readers of all ages, including *A Wrinkle in Time, Two-Part Invention, A Swiftly Tilting Planet, The Irrational Season,* and *The Glorious Impossible.*

MADELEINE L'ENGLE

There used to be great arguments about faith and work; you had to believe in one or the other. Many years ago my husband and I went to hear Rudolf Serkin playing an all Beethoven concert, and he played the "Sonata Appassionata" better than it could be played. It was absolutely incredible. People were standing on their seats, screaming and applauding, and I thought, Okay, that was a completely numinous, spirit-filled production. However, I'll bet Serkin practices the piano eight hours a day, every day, and if he didn't, this performance couldn't have happened. So in anything we do, unless we do our equivalent of that practicing, the Holy Spirit has nothing to work with. I know that when I am diligently at work, my work is good when I get out of the way and listen to God. I am still full of questions and movement in my understanding of the divine. But I do believe that nothing in art works well unless there is divine inspiration.

However, sometimes we don't know whether or not something was divinely inspired for decades. Van Gogh never knew, during his lifetime, that his paintings were divinely inspired, or that they were going to mean anything to anybody. I have on my desk, up in the country, an old cartoon from the old *Saturday Review* of a man dejectedly leaving a publisher's office with a big manuscript, and the publisher says: "We're very sorry, Mr. Tolstoy. We're just not in the market for a war book right now."

Many things that artists create are blocked by people or circumstances, not by God. For two and a half years I screamed at God because nobody wanted my book *A Wrinkle in Time.* It almost never got published. I kept saying, "It's a good book, a good book, I wrote it for you. Why all these rejection slips?" But we have to trust God's timing. *A Wrinkle in Time* came out at exactly the right moment, by publishers who did not expect it to be a success.

Neither the world nor the artist knows whether or not a work of art will last. The world often sees what it is told to see by the trends in the market at the time. Decisions are often made based on strategy and fear—on what is in vogue instead of on substance. The artist does not always know, does not always sense, whether or not the work has been divinely guided. William Faulkner once said, "I don't know anything about inspiration, because I don't know what inspiration is—I have heard about it, but I never saw it."[4]

Does this mean that those who do not feel inspiration have not received inspiration? Even those whose work has lasted over time?

Not everyone can feel or identify inspiration. Just as we do not always feel the love from someone who loves us, or feel a sense of trust from a person who trusts us, this does not mean that the love and trust were not there. Though we are wise to follow our instincts the majority of times, there are things at work that we do not always feel.

During our conversation with the artist and writer Faith Ringgold, she talked about how she senses a divine presence in work that has stood the test of time. She feels, as does Madeleine L'Engle, that it often takes years, or decades, to know whether or not one's work was divinely inspired. Ringgold was born in Harlem in 1930. She was influenced to use quilts as a medium for her paintings after hearing her mother's stories of slave ancestors who made quilts. Ringgold's quilts combine painting, quilted fabric, and storytelling. Her artwork has been exhibited in museums and galleries in the United States, Europe, Asia, South America, the Middle East, and Africa. She has published several children's books, which include, among others, *Tar Beach* and *My Dream of Martin Luther King*.

FAITH RINGGOLD

I sometimes look at my work when I have been away from it for a while, when it is no longer in exhibits, and I try to look back on it and remember how I created it. You plan it, you prepare it, you research it, you live with it, but it still seems at times as if the creation of the work just happens. Sometimes my hand is moving with the spirit of the project, and, hopefully, God is moving my hand. When this happens, I am connecting with God, and this connection empowers me.

There are times when I work that I have to stop what I am doing, concentrate, and pray in order to feel that connection with God.

When I was working on the cover for the book *My Dream of Martin Luther King,* nothing was coming to me. I went to my studio and I stayed there for a couple of days. I kept trying and trying, but it never felt right. Finally, I took a couple of hours and meditated on it, and then I prayed. I asked God to help me, and something helped me along. I was able to do the cover of King, and I think it was a very successful rendering of him. That connection with God is the most powerful connection there is. Many artists feel, when they are creating, that God is within them because they are making something from nothing. I always tell my students and other artists, "Don't wait to create whatever it is you feel inspired to create. Don't just think about it, do it. Do it now. You will look back on it years later, and find out whether or not it was good, or truly inspired. You can't find out what you did until you do it."

I was in Milan a few years ago. I had gone there to see "The Last Supper," and it was being restored at the time, so the room was very dark. There were so many people walking around, whispering, and trying to see the painting because they could feel that something important was there. This is true of all great paintings. They live because they continue to make that connection with people that the artist made with God.

To be filled with God's breath is our connection with God. Breath does not only fill us, it is also breathed out into the air we share with others. The divine breath that gives life to our work lives in the work beyond our vision of it, our creation of it, and long after it is finished and out of our hands. It continues to make a connection with people because it has a life of its own. It breathes out what has been breathed into it.

It has been said that the ideas that come to us when we create have a life of their own even *before* we begin the work. Mark Doty and Ang

Lee both observed that it seemed to them as if their ideas already existed and passed through them in order to be seen. The musician and composer Wynton Marsalis also has this sense of melodies already existing and passing through him. Marsalis made history in 1983 as the first artist to win Grammy awards in both the jazz and classical fields, an achievement he went on to repeat the following year. Since that time, Marsalis has won numerous Grammy and other awards, including the 1997 Pulitzer prize for his composition *Blood on the Fields,* an epic oratorio on slavery. This was the first Pulitzer ever awarded in the field of jazz.

WYNTON MARSALIS

Sometimes I wake up in the morning and I can just hear melodies and little themes, and I know that it's directly from God because it's pure, it's good, it just came through me. It doesn't happen with me a lot. With someone like Louis Armstrong—all the time. It depends on the musician. It depends on God.

My father is a jazz musician, and I have always practiced, but my inspiration comes from more than that. There are many people with fathers who are musicians, people who practice, but to understand— that's something else. Understanding comes from God. You can watch someone playing music, be inspired by what they're playing, and even if you're as talented, no matter how hard you try, you still couldn't play it that way for anything in the world. You ask, How did you do that? And the musician can tell you. It's obvious and clear to him. And when he shows you, it's clear, but when he's gone, you have no idea. How did he do it? He has the understanding that was given to him. You can develop an understanding, but the kernel has got to be given to you by God.

I pray when I play. Giving thanks to God can come in any form. You don't have to get on your knees and give thanks. When I'm truly grateful for something, I pray, and I pray when I don't have anything.

🔳

Throughout Scripture it is written that understanding comes from God. We see this in the verse that we keep coming back to, "There is a spirit in man: and the inspiration of the Almighty giveth them understanding" (Job 32:8). Proverbs 3:5–6 says, "Trust in the Lord with all thine heart; and lean not unto thine own understanding. In all thy ways acknowledge him, and he shall direct thy paths" (3:5,6).

When we acknowledge God as the one who gives us understanding, we will come to see that we create *with* God, not apart from Him. Understanding is a process. It takes time to see and to reflect on what God wants us to see. Our understanding and our talents are gifts from Him. It is not because of our will or our virtue that we receive these gifts. They come by grace, not because we have earned them. A devout believer may simply have been given less talent than a nonbeliever. A virtuous person may never produce the masterpiece that is produced by someone not virtuous at all.

Composer Steve Reich spoke to us about how he often finds there to be a contradiction between an artist and his work. Reich whose compositions include *Different Trains, Music for 18 Musicians,* and *The Cave,* is also composer of *Tehillim,* which was created after he began rediscovering Judaism through study and through observing religious rituals. In *Tehillim,* Reich utilized parts of four Psalms and cast them in the original, ancient biblical Hebrew. The piece begins with an excerpt from Psalm 19 ("The heavens declare the glory of God . . .") and concludes with verse 6 from Psalm 150 ("Let all that breathes praise the Eternal, Hallelujah").

STEVE REICH

✳

I don't generally think of inspiration in religious terms, or in divine terms, but I would say that there are so many things that we don't understand. Many of us wish to be spiritually uplifting, and to have our work come from a divine source, but I have questioned this because often you see such a huge contradiction when it comes to the artist and his work. Wagner wasn't a great guy, and he was a genius. You see this all the time, in all fields. You can produce work that appears to be divine, and you can still be a really horrible person. The opposite is also true. You can be a horrible artist, and a really wonderful guy.

Many musicians and composers feel, when things are really happening, that they're just vessels, that they can just kind of get out of the way and let the music come through, onto the paper, into the tape recorder, into the microphone, whatever it is. That's an inspired state. I've had this happen from time to time, but it doesn't happen frequently enough. Some of the pieces I composed were inspired by a Hebrew text, and certainly *Tehillim* was just that. I called it *Tehillim*, which is related to the word *hallelujah*, and is a setting of the Psalms, so people assumed it was religious music. I said, Well, no. And they said, What do you mean? I said, Well, for me, religious music means that it has a liturgical place. I would say that my source of inspiration was that I had put work and energy into learning about Judaism, and in observing the rituals of my religion, and there was a manifestation of all this in me as a composer. There's no question about that.

✳

It is sometimes difficult for us to reconcile that the artist is not the art. Wagner is a great example of an artist who appears inconsistent with his work. He was known as being nasty, self-focused, and an anti-Semite, and yet he was a musical genius who claimed, at certain points in life, to have had a deep Christian faith. Liszt was another composer whose art and spiritual practices seemed grossly inconsistent with his lifestyle. As a pianist, he was considered to be a virtuoso; as a man, he was considered to be a womanizer; and as a man of faith, he was considered to be a devout believer who entered the priesthood when he was in his fifties, and who credited his musical inspiration to God.

These men, of course, were human, with talents and failings. After years of persecuting Christians, Saint Paul was transformed into the man who wrote: "Love is patient, love is kind. It does not envy, it does not boast, it is not proud. It is not rude, it is not self-seeking, it is not easily angered, it keeps no record of wrongs. Love does not delight in evil but rejoices with the truth. It always protects, always trusts, always hopes, always perseveres" (1 Corinthians:13:4–7—NIV).

If we replaced the word *love,* or the word *it* with our name, if we said, "Paul is patient, Paul is kind, Paul does not envy," not one of us, including Paul, could say that everything on the list was entirely true of who we are. Not even the most virtuous one of us. We are all inconsistent, we all have our failings, and God inspires us anyway.

When Reich said that from focusing on his religion there was a manifestation of this in him as a composer, we are again reminded that our creative vision is often colored by the way we have come to see the world. During our conversation with the children's author Katherine Paterson, she said that the Bible has influenced who she is as a person and as an author. Paterson is the author of *The Great Gilly Hopkins, Bridge to Terabithia, Jacob Have I Loved,* and *Lyddie.* She has won two Newbery Medals and two National Book Awards.

KATHERINE PATERSON

The Bible was the most formative literary influence on my entire life. Was and is. I was raised on the King James Bible, which is lovely for language as well as for all kinds of other things. It's the way I see the world. It's how I view truth. And those stories are my stories. I am Jacob in the wilderness, dreaming of the ladder, going up and down. I'm Jacob wrestling with the angel. I'm Joseph, who shows off and raises the envy of his brothers. And those are the stories, bone of my bone and flesh of my flesh. I couldn't be myself or a writer apart from the Bible.

I think we are all meant to be creative because we were made in the image of the Creator. When I walk into my study, I'm involved in something that's larger than myself. I receive inspiration as I work. It is all grace, and all work. On the one hand, inspiration is a gift, and on the other, it comes when you are doing the hardest work you could possibly do. The creative process is a mystery. Every time I finish a book I feel that I'll never write another one. Then the seeds of the next book come in various ways because you do not write a book based on a single idea, or course, you write it based on a complex of ideas. It takes patience to wait for the knitting together of those ideas.

If I look back at something that I've done, and realize that it's better than I remembered or than I could have done on my own, then I really do feel that there is a providence in my life, that I have been given work to do in order to have a voice to say something that God wants me to say. Now, God doesn't line me up and say, "This is what I want you to write." Part of what I have to do is to figure out what it is He wants. Flannery O'Connor once said that fiction isn't an incarnation of art, it is the word becoming flesh. It is the word coming into human experience. And I find the whole notion of incarnation very powerful. It is God with us and, for me, God with us in Jesus that I find so important.

鈴

The Word in Scripture, just as the word in fiction, is, as Paterson put it, the word coming into human experience. Most of what we read in the Bible is told through poems and stories and parables, and we relate what we read to our lives. It is only by seeing what we read in relation to our lives that it may move us as a Word of God. The writer who writes fiction knows that the word must come into human experience if it is to move us at all. We must be able to relate it to our lives. It must seem true—not factual, but true. Though literature, unlike the Bible, is not considered to be divine, if it is inspired we may see the divine in it.

Author Kathleen Norris told us, "When you write, you're not just in a dialogue with yourself. You're really in a dialogue with the world, and if you have some faith that the world was created, or is part of a divine being, then you know that you are in a dialogue with the divine."

Norris is the author of *The Cloister Walk, Dakota: A Spiritual Geography, Amazing Grace: A Vocabulary of Faith,* and three volumes of poetry. Though she was raised as a Presbyterian, Norris became, and has been, a Benedictine oblate of Assumption Abbey in North Dakota for over a decade. In what follows, Norris discusses how she feels she has "been able to integrate poetic inspiration and divine inspiration" in her life.

KATHLEEN NORRIS

When I wrote *The Cloister Walk*, what had astonished me so much was that as I immersed myself more and more in the traditional monastic liturgy, which is really the traditional liturgies of the Christian church—the daily Liturgies of the Hours, morning to evening taken up with certain hours of prayer—the whole thing struck me as a kind of poem. I was, in a sense, part of a living poem, and it wasn't one that I had made up. This enriched my whole sense of what the poetic vocation is, and what inspiration is in general. I had long thought of religion as dead, as not part of my life, and it amazes me that I have been able to integrate poetic inspiration and divine inspiration—two areas of my life that I had thought were pretty far apart. Some of the newer poems that I have written have been in direct response to monastic literature, which really means a direct response to the Bible.

I try to write and pray every day. I do my best writing and praying in the morning, when I'm quiet and not distracted, and when I'm away from the phone, the fax, and the TV. Being quiet helps me to be receptive to inspiration. My mind starts to fill with ideas or even lines of verse. A quiet activity that is perfectly compatible with poetry is baking bread because you start out with something small, you mix it together, and then there's this period of waiting for the bread to rise. Waiting is a big part of any artistic or spiritual discipline. You're not going to get everything right, right away. You have to wait for things to come to completion.

In Scripture, Jesus tells his disciples the parable of the growing seed. Jesus said, "This is what the kingdom of God is like. A man scatters seed on the ground. Night and day, whether he sleeps or gets up, the seed sprouts and grows, though he does not know how. All by itself the soil produces grain—first the stalk, then the head, then the full kernel in the head. As soon as the grain is ripe, he puts the sickle to it, because the harvest has come" (Mark 4:26–29—NIV).

Whether it be in what we create, or in what we pray for, we are waiting for the harvest. Sarah and Abraham waited decades to have the child God had promised them. The *Ring* cycle *(Der Ring des Nibelungen)* took Wagner twenty years to compose. We sit with our work, waiting. We seek God, waiting. We wait for an answer, a sign, understanding and sight. We wait for something to fill us and pass through us. And yet, something is at work, whether we see it or not, just as we cannot see ourselves grow, or feel ourselves breathe as we are sleeping.

PRAYER

IN DIALOGUE WITH GOD

I remember praying as a kid, and I prayed like a scientist. I wanted God to prove God's existence to me. I would pray and hear silence, and be convinced that if there were silence, the whole thing didn't work. I watched Davey and Goliath *a lot, which was this claymation religious program on television, and in that show God was always yelling stuff out. God was a real chatty guy. So, as a kid, I couldn't put those two things together. I would say now, though, that silence seems divine to me, and to pray and hear silence is a beautiful thing, a really compelling image. But, as a kid, I wanted it to be like long distance—you pray, and someone talks back and answers your questions.*

RICK MOODY

So often we exchange silence. Put us in a public place with people we don't know, and we comfortably avoid one another. I once sat with people I didn't know, for seven hours, in the waiting room of Memorial Sloan-Kettering Hospital. This hospital treats many forms of one disease. Every patient has, or is being tested for, cancer. I waited there, with strangers, to hear about my mother. For hours, none of us who waited addressed one another. This seemed appropriate, this silence. We did not want to know any more than we had to know. And, in that context, we did not want to be known.

And yet, at some point, toward the end of that wait, a few of us said a few words. We might have said we were tired or concerned, I don't remember exactly what, but whatever we said broke the silence.

In *The Magnificent Defeat,* Frederick Buechner wrote:

This is what I think, in essence, prayer is. It is the breaking of silence. It is the need to be known and the need to know. Prayer is the sound made by our deepest aloneness. I am thinking not just of formal prayers that a religious person might say in church or in bed at night, but of the kind of vestigial, broken fragments of prayer that people use without thinking of them as prayers: something terrible happens, and you might say, 'God help us,' or 'Jesus Christ'—the poor, crippled prayers that are hidden in the minor blasphemies of people for whom in every sense God is dead except that they still have to speak to him if only through clenched teeth. Prayer is a man's impulse to open up his life at its deepest level.

People pray because they cannot help it. In one way or another, I think, all people pray.[1]

My mother has said that she does not pray or believe in God, but as it turned out, in the hospital, as she was being wheeled in for surgery, she was approached by a nun. The nun offered to pray for her, and my mother accepted. The nun prayed, "May the Lord guide the surgeon's hand." It also turned out that a friend of my mother's was scheduled to have an "audience" with the pope, in Rome, a few days before my mother's operation. After my mother came home, she received a card with her name on it, a blessing from the pope, and his photograph. For the past two years, during which she has been in remission, my mother has kept this card.

Many people—even nonbelievers—turn to prayer when they are desperate. We may not know who or what God is, or to what degree we believe, but deep down we know that there is something operating in the universe that is beyond what we can see. Prayer is first, for most people, an expression of need. Whether we want or yearn in silence or aloud, our wants and yearnings come from our spirits. In places like hospitals, we are faced with the limits of what we can control. Our yearnings become prayers when we ask for help.

Many of us who do ask consider prayer to be private. To pray where others might see you, other than in temple or church—to be seen bowing, or kneeling, or to be heard saying the words—can, for many people, be embarrassing. It is sometimes even awkward to hear *ourselves* say the words. But whether we pray in private or in public, there is no set way to pray. In Scripture, Abraham bowed and prayed to God in front of three men who appeared in the tent door where he sat. Solomon "kneeled down upon his knees before all the congregation of Israel" and prayed (2 Chronicles 6:13). Jesus, in front of his disciples, "fell on his face, and prayed" (Matthew 26:39), and He also prayed in isolation, in a "solitary place" (Mark 1:35). Jonah prayed alone from inside a fish.

Where we are, how we pose, which words we say are details that vary. They matter less than that our prayers give us peace. We pray to God believing or hoping that He will help us, that He is beyond the limits of what we can control. We pray to have our needs met, to be guided, healed, and inspired. Through prayer, we enter into a dialogue with God. None of us would pray if we did not believe, or think there was a chance, that God would listen and in some way respond—not in our time, not in our way, but in some divine way. When we persist in prayer we are in what Diana Eck refers to as an "ongoing conversation."

DIANA ECK

I do feel a strong sense of God's presence and inspiration. I feel my own opening to God, through song and the kind of ongoing conversation that I refer to as prayer. The prayers that I return to are the Lord's Prayer, the Twenty-third Psalm, and the brief form of prayer that is associated with the Jesus prayer, "Lord Jesus Christ, have mercy, be present." There are a lot of hymns in the Christian tradition that are like prayers, and are associated with the Spirit. Coming from a Methodist, hymn-singing background, I return to them again and again, walking to work, for example. "Breathe on Me, Breath of God" is one of them.

> *Breathe on me, Breath of God*
> *Fill me with life anew,*
> *That I may love what Thou dost love,*
> *And do what Thou wouldst do.*
>
> *Breathe on me, Breath of God*
> *Till I am wholly Thine*

Till all this earthly part of me
Glows with Thy fire divine.

With that verse I inevitably think of the fires of Manikarnika, the cremation grounds in Banaras. It is a reminder of both the gift of life and its certain consummation.

Inspiration is not some extraordinary experience. It is what grounds the whole of my life. It is like the soil of life, the breath of life itself. I don't believe that the one I call God tinkers in every step of my life, or tells me how I am going to deal with this situation or that situation. I don't experience God as a micromanager in my life. However, I experience an opening to God, and a general sense of guidance through prayer on a day-to-day basis. Beyond words, I also need to sink deeply into silence or meditation to experience the openness that is without the continual chatter of my own mind, and without the thinking through of daily events that can so overtake us. Our spiritual lives begin with something as simple as being present, and paying attention. As our lives become busier, distraction becomes a serious spiritual challenge. We need to exercise that capacity to be present, just as much as we need to practice in order to play a musical instrument. As time goes on, we will become less distracted in our capacity for attention, and stronger, as a result, in compassion.

We must be present to be in dialogue. It is not always easy to keep our minds from wandering, to keep ourselves from being preoccupied with thoughts about the future or the past. When we are distracted, we are not really listening, not really intimate, not really there. This is true of how we relate to people as well as how we relate to God. In the Gospels we read the story of when Jesus came to the home of Martha and her sister Mary. Martha was so focused on what she had to prepare, and serve, and do that she nearly lost sight of Jesus. Mary, on the other hand, sat by Jesus, and listened to what He said. When Martha complained to Jesus, "Lord, dost thou not care that my sister hath left me to serve alone? bid her therefore that she help me" (Luke 10:40), Jesus responded by saying, "Martha, Martha, thou art careful and troubled about many things. But one thing is needful, and Mary hath chosen that good part, which shall not be taken away from her" (Luke 10:41,42).

We are often so overcome with the events in our lives that without realizing what we are doing, or meaning to, we lose sight of more "needful" things. We become quick to lose perspective, and to justify our perspective, even when what is "needful" is right in front of us. When this happens, we are often caught off guard. This is not what we had planned or intended. How often do we have every intention of being fully engaged, and then find ourselves drifting away?

This is often what happens when we pray. The thoughts that tick away in our brains keep us from being present—present as we speak, and as we wait for God's response. People who meditate try to focus on a word, or on their breath, so that the mind does not drift away but stays focused. When we quiet ourselves, we learn to listen.

> *Be still before the Lord and wait patiently for Him*
> *(Psalm 37:7—NIV)*
> *Be still, and know that I am God*
> *(Psalm 46:10)*

When we pray, we worship, praise, confess, intercede for others, but most of us come to prayer with requests. We pray for health, strength, and protection. We pray to be spared a loss. We pray when we are discouraged, anxious, impatient, and fed up, when we want something in our lives to change. When we are lonely, we pray for a person—a spouse, a child. We pray to be loving, and to be loved. We pray for more money, a better job, a better house, better *things*. When we are confused, we pray to see clearly, and to make sense of what we see. We pray for guidance and inspiration.

Prayer is not magical. We do not always get what we pray for. We do not receive inspiration every time we pray. Inspiration is a gift, a grace, a mystery. And yet, by praying, we are more likely to be open to God's grace, more open, when it comes, to receiving it.

MADELEINE L'ENGLE

One of my daily prayers is "Please help me to serve my work well." Then I name the book that I am working on and say, "Please let it be for you, for love."

ANDRE DUBUS

"Help me to write well of you, and for you."

RICK MOODY

I pray before I work. In fact, when I was writing *The Ice Storm*, I would pray every day in a very specific way. I would say, "I don't know what I am doing with this book. Please help me do it." I felt what I was trying to do was to be part of the tradition of invoking what you find in epic poetry, like what Milton says at the beginning of *Paradise Lost*, something like "This poet is inadequate to the task. Fill him with your voice." I feel that is what I'm trying to do with my work. I see it as requiring prayers in order to activate it in some way. I'm trying to get God to prompt me to do what I do, in the same way that some singers say that they feel moved by God to sing.

KATHLEEN NORRIS

One of the reasons that learning the Psalms the way you do when you pray them every day in a monastery is really quite helpful is because sometimes, if you are frightened, or busy, or just distracted, those lines of the Psalms will just pop into your mind and guide you. And that is inspiration. A prayer that pops into my mind quite often is a verse that begins Psalm 70. "Make haste, O God to deliver me; make haste to help me, O Lord." Basically, this translates as *HELP!*

FAITH RINGGOLD

I don't pray specific prayers anymore. When I was a child, we used to have to say our prayers every night—"Now I lay me down to sleep, I pray the Lord my soul to keep." Now, when I feel I really need something, I say a little prayer. I'll say something like "O God, please help me to do this, or help me to get through this." Every time I'm doing a lecture somewhere, and I really want to communicate with that particular audience, I always say to myself, "O God, help me to communicate what it is I have in mind to these people. Help me to connect with them." And then I can feel the connection coming on. I pray all the time that I am able to do that.

JOHN POLKINGHORNE

A prayer that I use is one of the Collects from The Book of Common Prayer, which says, "O God, forasmuch as without thee we are not able to please thee, mercifully grant that thy Holy Spirit may in all things direct and rule our hearts" (Proper 19). In other words, grant that God's spirit will inspire us. I want God's blessing and spirit, so that is a prayer I use a great deal.

LEONTYNE PRICE

I like to pray when I first wake up, to thank Him for another day. I never perform without praying. There's a joke about me that refers to the very important time in my life, back in 1961, when I made my debut at the Metropolitan Opera House. I guess I must have been a pioneer because I prayed before going on stage. That night I had to say to the stagehand who was telling me to go on, "Wait a minute. I have something to do that's more important than anything. In other words, it has to do with whether the show goes on or not." That was such an overwhelming evening for me, and I remember praying, "I wouldn't be here if you didn't arrange it, and I really need you to get me through the next four acts."

A friend of mine told a joke that she had heard her rabbi tell during one of his sermons. A woman is walking on the beach with her daughter on a very windy day. The girl impulsively runs into the water, and the undertow pulls her in. When she is out of sight, the mother pleads to God, "O God, please save my daughter. She is my only daughter, my only child. I am begging you, please don't let her drown. I will never, for the rest of my life, ask for one other thing. She is all that I want. Please, God, I beg you, save her." Suddenly, the wind calms down, and the mother sees the girl. She runs to her daughter and looks up at God. "She had a hat," the mother says.

Is there anything too small to pray about? Though we tend to feel that it is most valid to pray for matters of life and death, no need, when it is our need, feels small. It seems that we often look up at God and pray for our equivalent of that hat. In Scripture, we are told to pray for *everything*. In *everything* "let your requests be made known unto God" (Philippians 4:6). Just as we are sometimes so drawn to someone that, in a rush, without even knowing the person well, we will find ourselves confiding in him or her about anything, we do the same with God when we pray. In *The Varieties of Religious Experience,* William James wrote that the act of prayer is "the very movement itself of the soul, putting itself in a personal relation of contact with the mysterious power of which it feels the presence—it may be even before it has a name by which to call it."[2]

We don't always know what to call the mysterious power that draws us to someone, that compels us to open up to this person the deepest part of who we are. Is it love, or intimacy, or a false sense of both? Whatever it is, whatever opens us to a person, or to God, it is a pull so strong that we cannot help ourselves from revealing the largest and smallest things. Christopher Parkening talked about this pull to pray about even the smallest things.

CHRISTOPHER PARKENING

I pray, if for no other reason than to commune with God, and to learn to submit, to learn to line up my will with His will, and to rejoice in that process. I guess prayer would become presumption if I didn't say to God, "Whatever would give you the greatest glory, whatever would advance your name, whatever would give you honor, with my music and my life, that's what I want to do." I try and close many of my prayers with the Lord's Prayer.

I have also learned to pray about the smallest of things. I pray before every concert. I ask that He be glorified. I dedicate the concert to Him. I ask that He would have the people hear what He wants them to hear. I ask that He would keep any evil influence away. I ask that I trust Him and have the right attitude as I play. A great comfort to me is the Philippians passage in chapter 4 which says, "Be careful for nothing; but in every thing by prayer and supplication with thanksgiving let your requests be made known unto God. And the peace of God, which passeth all understanding, shall keep your hearts and minds through Christ Jesus" (4:6,7). The peace comes not because your prayer has been answered exactly as you prayed it, but because you have shifted your focus and the burden of responsibility on to Him.

There's a story I often tell, about the time I performed on the Grammy awards with Kathleen Battle, and we were just about to play, and we came out at a commercial break. You look down at the first row, and you see Michael Jackson, Dionne Warwick, Barbra Streisand, Paul Simon, Stevie Wonder, and on and on, and eight thousand five hundred people at the Shrine Auditorium in Los Angeles. Of course, it was being taped live for CBS and aired around the world.

And the fellow with the headset was standing next to me, and he said, "Mr. Parkening, we have twenty seconds till air." And I said, "Fine." And then he said, "Well, in twenty seconds you'll be performing for over two hundred million people—live." I thought the timing of that remark was not the greatest, but I looked up at Kathy (we had prayed just before going out) and I said, "The only thing for us to do is to play and sing for the Lord, right?" And she said, "Right." That gave us a peace that we would not have known if we tried to "impress" the people and play for them.

To play for God, just as to pray to God, means that we turn the focus of our attention to Him. When we focus on anything with the hope of nurturing it, we tend to focus on it consistently. Every day, or as consistently as they can, musicians play, dancers dance, writers write, and parents parent. People pray daily, or as consistently as they can, so that they might deepen and nurture their faith. We are not always motivated or inspired to pray each day, or to play music, to dance, or to write. To get ourselves to do these things daily involves discipline. Often it is *during* our work and our prayers that inspiration comes. With consistent practice and focus, there is more likely to be progress, inspiration, and depth.

If prayer, as Frederick Buechner put it, "is the need to be known and the need to know," that need is as consistent as our prayers are. Many people who pray daily, daily want to know the nature of God. There are those who come to prayer with requests, and part of what they request is that they would find Him, know Him, that He would reveal Himself to them.

MARK RICHARD

It is so hard for me to remember to pray daily. As a writer, you have such an unstructured life, or at least mine is, so sometimes I stay up all night working, or I get up early and forget. But when I pray, I always try to say, "Please let me do good work in your name." That's the most important thing. If my work is going to be self-serving, I really don't want to do it. The other thing I pray for is that God would reveal Himself to me.

JOHN POLKINGHORNE

There are certain prayers that I pray daily. Because I am very moved by the passion of Christ, I pray the prayer of Sir Richard of Chichester—"Thanks be to you, my Lord Jesus Christ, for all the grief and sorrows, pain and insults you have borne for us. Our best redeemer, friend, and brother, may we know you more clearly, love you more dearly, and follow you more nearly, day by day."

We want to know God, who He is. We want to know if He can hear us, and if He will respond. We want to know who we are asking to know us.

Thomas Merton put it this way, in *Thoughts in Solitude,* when writing about contemplative prayer: "The only thing to seek in contemplative prayer is God, and we seek Him successfully when we realize that we cannot find Him unless He shows Himself to us, and yet, at the same time, that He would not have inspired us to seek Him unless we had already found Him."[3]

Often by feeling the presence of God's Spirit can we know Him. It is not always by knowledge that we know Him, but by expressions of His love. During our conversation with Reverend Jean-Pierre Ruiz, a Roman Catholic priest of the diocese of Brooklyn, New York, he talked about how it is through the presence of God that he comes to know himself. Ruiz teaches in the Department of Theology and Religious Studies at St. John's University, in Jamaica, New York. He is the editor in chief of the *Journal of Hispanic/Latino Theology,* and is active in interreligious concerns and organizations.

REVEREND
JEAN-PIERRE RUIZ

One of the most important parts of my daily routine is the Liturgy of the Hours, which is a prayer that is required of the Roman Catholic clergy, and it consists of the praying of the Psalms and other texts from Scripture at several points during the course of the day—from the morning prayer to the night prayer. It is a daily cycle and an annual cycle that invites the presence of God into my life. I find that praying the Psalms in the Liturgy of the Hours helps me to be aware of—and to be responsive to—the presence of God, and to learn about the purpose of my life in God's care, and in God's purpose. Sometimes it feels as if nothing is happening, but I am there. I think it was Flannery O'Connor who said that, when she wrote, she sat at her typewriter for hours every morning, and if something happened, that that was fine, and if nothing happened, then she just sat there anyway. Sometimes I just sit. And sometimes, by contrast, when I sit there is an energy, a drive, a subtle inspiration to do whatever that day is going to bring, a real sense of purpose and of the presence of God.

❖

It is only by listening that we can be guided. When we pray, we sense in our spirits what words to say. We sense God's response, and what direction to take. His purpose for us, if we are listening, becomes ours.

We are not led on one straight line to one particular path. We are often led, in different directions, to many paths. At the age of thirteen, Thomas Moore left his home in Detroit to prepare for the priesthood at a Catholic prep seminary. The seminary was also a monastery, and Moore lived there as a monk for twelve years. Shortly before he was to be ordained, Moore decided to leave the seminary. "This was the 1960s," he said, during our interview. "There was a lot of change in the air, and I think that affected me. I was doing a lot of reading, and I was being exposed to interesting ideas and people." Moore went on to college, and then to graduate school, where he received degrees in theology, musicology, and philosophy. From 1976 to 1983 Moore was a professor of religion and psychology at Southern Methodist University. He practiced psychotherapy in private practice until 1991.

The 1992 publication of his book *Care of the Soul (A Guide for Cultivating Depth and Sacredness in Everyday Life)* changed the course of his life. *Care of the Soul* stayed on *The New York Times* bestseller list for forty-four weeks, and went on to become the number-one bestseller in paperback for 145 weeks.

"Suddenly," Moore says, "I wrote a book that millions of people read. Before that, only dozens of people had read what I wrote. And that had nothing to do with my intention or control. To me it is a mystery that my life changed quite radically with a publication of a book that I really didn't think anyone would care to read."

The follow-up to *Care of the Soul,* 1994's *Soul Mates: Honoring the Mysteries of Love and Relationship,* was another bestseller, and solidified Moore's reputation as a spiritual writer. He is now a leading lecturer in North America and Europe in the areas of archetypal psychology, mythology, and the imagination.

THOMAS MOORE

Being raised with my Catholic background, I return to the Hail Mary and the Lord's Prayer all the time. It's interesting because when I was a young man, from twelve years old to the time I was twenty-five, I woke up at five-fifteen every morning to somebody knocking on my door saying "Ave Maria."

> *Hail Mary, full of grace*
> *The Lord is with you*
> *Blessed are you among women,*
> *and blessed is the fruit of your womb, Jesus*
> *Holy Mary, Mother of God,*
> *Pray for us, sinners,*
> *Now and at the hour of our death.*
> *Amen.*

This prayer, the Ave Maria, the Hail Mary, comes from the Annunciation. It's one of the most remarkable prayers I have ever encountered—not only because of its poetry, but because of the mystery of the Annunciation. For many years I have been fascinated by the image of the Annunciation. It's something I meditate on and write about a lot. Whenever I go to an art museum, I will spend an inordinate amount of time in front of a fifteenth-century Annunciation. I find myself being drawn to that image over and over again. One of the key moments in the Annunciation is when the angel tells the Virgin Mary that she will be pregnant with the divine *thing*. The angel says in Greek the word *thing*. Some *thing* that is divine. And Mary says, "Let it be done, as you say, according to your word." Her faith seems to be something from another world, beyond what I could grasp or understand.

I feel very much that I am not in control of the shape of my life. I don't mean that I don't make decisions, but I think that there is definitely *providence*. That is the word I learned in the Catholic theology. Divine providence means that there is a destiny. My life has not taken a straight line. I have gone in many different directions. The most difficult experiences for me have been, first, to have gotten divorced, and then to have had another experience of something like divorce to someone I was not actually married to, but very close to. To have two long-standing relationships end tested me more than almost anything, in the sense of wondering what was the right thing to do, and feeling the tremendous loss.

I had a lesser challenge when I was denied tenure at the university where I was teaching about fifteen years ago. Everything I had been preparing to do, and everything I wanted—teaching college—was taken away from me. I didn't know where to go next. I still hold the terrible feelings of loss, and of the changes that happened then. But in all those instances, I have discovered that the way the future unfolded was quite wonderful.

I grew up learning that God is an infinite mystery. I have been taught to place my faith in something other than the very limited events around me. I look for direction and meaning much beyond human wisdom and prudence. And so, in a sense, whenever I respond to something that I don't fully understand and say, "Yes, I will do that," there is an element in this that is like the Annunciation.

To make requests, in prayer, is only part of prayer. We not only ask, and then sense God's response within the silence, we also respond to what we sense—whether we understand or not. Or, like Mary, we may hear and respond to something we did not ask for. What God communicates does not force us, but *empowers* us, to respond. It is not as if we salute, follow orders, and make an about-face in our lives on command. We are not *required* to follow what we hear. When we follow, we choose to go.

Beyond praying for ourselves, we also make prayer requests on behalf of others. We pray for our family and friends. We are prayed for by our rabbi, minister, or priest. Our request, in prayer, is referred to as our petition. Our request for others is known as intercessory prayer. It is our act of asking for help for someone else.

RABBI ALEXANDER SCHINDLER

I see prayer as being communally strengthening. When I pray, I ask God to bring strength to other people. And in turn, when I come to a synagogue with serious problems—I'm worried about a child who is ill, or I feel bereft because my father died—the fact that I'm at that worship service, and surrounded by people who seek to comfort me by their presence, my pain is eased. To pray regularly takes discipline. People say, "Oh, I can pray in a barn," but most of the people who tell me this haven't gone to their barn lately.

FAITH RINGGOLD

I have a friend whose child is sick, and it is a very serious condition. I say a prayer for my friend and for her child every day. I say, "God, please help her daughter, help her daughter to be open to you." I ask God to help me to be there for those two, and for Him to help the child, help the mother, help all of us.

We expect certain people to intervene for us, but not in terms of prayer. We expect lawyers to defend us in court, and doctors to help us improve our health. And yet, there are professionals who believe that their prayers add to their help.

Dr. Michael E. DeBakey is a surgeon who is internationally recognized for his achievements and innovations in the area of cardiovascular health. He has been an advisor to almost every United States president in the past fifty years, and to heads of state throughout the world.

MICHAEL E. DEBAKEY, M.D.

As a surgeon, I have witnessed what seemed like a miracle in the recovery of patients when all scientific evidence pointed to the opposite. I have, myself, seemed impelled to continue trying to save a patient when it seemed futile, and have been overjoyed when the patient recovered, despite overwhelming odds. At such times, one

cannot help feeling strongly that there is a supreme being who inter-
vened. What other explanation is there?

Practicing Christian physicians do not necessarily kneel and pray
as they administer to their patients. It is, rather, a matter of commun-
ing with God on a continuous basis. God guides us; we are his instruments.

The Maimonides Prayer for the Physician begins: "Exalted God—
before I begin the holy work of healing the creations of your hands, I
place my entreaty before the throne of your glory that you grant
strength of spirit and fortitude to faithfully execute my work."

This is a prayer of both petition and intercession, for it is a prayer
that requests strength for the person praying, in relation to his or her
work, and at the same time, the work that is being done is done for
others. This prayer asks that God will use the person praying as a
vessel through which the healing of others will take place.

When we pray, or ask God to use us as a vessel to pray for others,
often that vessel is filled with our own fears and doubts. We may be
anxious about what we are praying for. We may doubt the way we
pray. We may doubt God, that He will help us. And yet, as we pray,
despite our doubts, our fears turn to peace as we sense God's presence. We build up a sense of faith. Often a healing takes place in
ourselves as we pray for the healing of others.

Prayer calls on God's Spirit, the breath of life. We pray for divine
intervention, and sometimes it comes—the healing that seems like a
miracle. Yet this is not to say that healing comes *only* to people who
pray, or *only* to people who have been prayed for by others. This
would imply that patients who did not have faith, or did not have
people praying for them, would not be likely to recover. This, of
course, is not true. Certainly those who do not pray have recovered
from life-threatening diseases. Likewise, healing does not always come

to people who pray even the most passionate prayers. Paul pleaded three times that God would remove the thorn from his flesh, but God did not oblige Paul. Though Jesus prayed to be spared his fate in the Garden of Gethsemane, God had a different plan.

In the chapter "Loss, Grief, and Healing: Where Is God?" we observed that things happen in the world that are not caused by us or by God. Our bodies are human and imperfect. Even the healthiest person gets ill. Even the strongest person sometimes does not recover. Our faith, or lack of faith, does not spare us from these realities, or cause them.

When neither a miracle nor medicine heals us, divine inspiration will. Not our bodies, but our spirits. When we are empowered with God's strength to persevere, we are healed, whether our bodies are healed or not.

Sometimes we intercede for others, when we witness life treating them unfairly, by arguing with God. This notion of arguing with God came up during our interview with the noted lawyer Alan Dershowitz. Dershowitz is a professor at Harvard Law School, and the author of the bestsellers *Chutzpah, Reversal of Fortune,* and *Reasonable Doubts: The Criminal Justice System and the O. J. Simpson Case.* Dershowitz lectures widely on issues such as anti-Semitism, cultural identity, the Holocaust, assimilation, and Israeli-U.S. relations. He teaches a seminar at Harvard Law School on the biblical concepts of justice. "The thesis of my course," Dershowitz told us, "is that holy books, religious books, including the Old Testament, the New Testament, and the Qur'an, have an enormous influence on our secular concepts of justice, and on the daily life of people in all societies."

A L A N   M .   D E R S H O W I T Z

I was born in Brooklyn, New York, into a very religious, Orthodox
Jewish family. The center of my life was religious observance. I prayed
every single day, three times a day. Every Saturday I went to the
synagogue with my parents, and my brother, and my grandmother,
and we ate only kosher food, and complied with all the basic rules of
Orthodox Judaism. The first thirteen years of my education, from
kindergarten through high school, were all religious education. I studied Torah thoroughly. I studied the prophets, the Talmud, and the
rules of Judaism. During those years, I learned about justice, about
the imperfect human quest for justice.

In the Bible, there are many stories in which there is a debate
between the Jews and God over issues of justice. The first Bible story
that inspired me, and continues to inspire me, is the story of Abraham
arguing with God over whether God would kill all the people of
Sodom and Gomorrah, or only the guilty people. The obvious question that would jump into anybody's mind is, Why would so many
innocent people have to be killed? Now, it turned out that Abraham
changed God's mind and persuaded God not to kill the innocent
people of Sodom. In fact, Abraham said to God, in effect, "How dare
you kill innocent people." What the Bible tells us is that God accepted an argument from a human being, and He was persuaded by a
human being. So what Judaism gave me, right from the beginning,
was permission to argue with God.

I think about God all the time. I experience a very personal relationship with Him. That relationship doesn't go through the rabbi, it
doesn't go through Moses, it doesn't go through the experience at
Sinai. It is a very personal relationship, and it is an argumentative,
personal relationship. There is actually a verse in the Talmud where

somebody argues with God about an obscure point—about the cleanliness of an oven. In the end, the Talmud said that God turned to the angels and said, "My children have defeated me in argument." There aren't too many traditions which include God acknowledging defeat at the hands of human beings in argument.

I argue with God over issues like the Holocaust and AIDS, but I realize that I don't understand all that I see—those human experiences that are incomprehensible to human beings. Why would God give human beings intelligence and the ability to doubt, unless He wanted us to go through various phases. My inspiration has always come from being in a dialogue with God.

Like Dershowitz, author Madeleine L'Engle has argued with God on behalf of others. She has said that when things seem unjust, and she argues with God, her argument is still a prayer.

MADELEINE L'ENGLE

I pray all the time, whether I pray well or not. I have sometimes felt closest to God when I have been furious. For instance, when my mother was ninety, she started spiraling downhill. She had been a brilliant, wonderful woman, and I was absolutely furious about what was happening to her. I would take the dogs for a walk, and I would say to God, "Don't do this to my mother. You take her." And God took her. Now, that was prayer. It wasn't a very good prayer, but it was prayer.

There are also prayers that we pray in acceptance of what seems unfair. When faced with a death, a loss, one might experience a crisis of faith. However, those who pray the Mourner's Kaddish say this prayer to *declare* their faith. It is a prayer in which, despite our loss, our sorrow, God is the subject of praise. It is also a prayer that seeks to honor the dead, and the bond between the dead and the living:

THE MOURNER'S KADDISH

Let the glory of God be extolled, let His great name be hallowed in the world whose creation He willed. May His kingdom soon prevail, in our own day, our own lives, and the life of all Israel, and let us say: Amen.

Let His great name be blessed for ever and ever. Let the name of the Holy One, blessed is He, be glorified, exalted, and honored, though He is beyond all the praises, songs, and adorations that we can utter, and let us say: Amen. For us and for all Israel, may the blessing of peace and the promise of life come true, and let us say: Amen.

MONICA CHUSID

I believe that when you say the Mourner's Kaddish, you are glorifying God's kingdom, because it is not a prayer about death, it is a prayer that reaffirms life. You are reaffirming that you still have a life to live, and that you, as a mourner, can be there for someone else. I try to do that. It is difficult sometimes because it brings you right back to that place again, to that pain, but I believe that this is the best thing I can do because I have to take my loss and make something out of it, like being there to comfort someone else.

BENJAMIN HIRSCH

I feel led to pray for people who died in the Holocaust. Many of them have no one to say Kaddish for them, so I say Kaddish every day. The Kaddish is a prayer of praise for God. Traditionally, Kaddish is said during the first year after someone has passed away. By praising God in the name of someone else, you are trying to elevate the soul of the person that you are saying Kaddish for. I feel good doing that, knowing that someone I don't even know is having his soul elevated by this prayer. So it gives me a reason to get up early and go to synagogue every morning.

Believing that someone might benefit from our prayers is what inspires many people to pray. And at times, people become inspired simply by knowing that they are being prayed for. During our conversation with Desmond Tutu, the archbishop of South Africa, he spoke about prayer.

DESMOND TUTU

One important thing about prayer is that, particularly at those times when our spiritual resources appear to have vanished, and we are really low, the Church is praying. If I am feeling awful, and my prayer is thoroughly unexciting, and probably useless, I am then able to throw myself into the arms of the Church, and into the worship and adoration of far holier people, and into the prayer of the Church in and through our great high priest, Jesus Christ. The ongoing paeans of praise and adoration ascend to the heavenly throne, almost like a river. I just throw myself in, and allow the current to carry me. I would be totally useless without Mother Church, without my fellow Christians, and without the head of the Church, Jesus Christ. So, for instance, when you are dead exhausted, and you are wanting to pray but cannot bring yourself to concentrate for one moment because of all sorts of distractions, you can say, at that point, God, I want to worship you, to adore you, to praise you, to love you, but you know that I'm feeling like death warmed up. So, you can just throw yourself into this perfect act of worship that is offered by Jesus Christ, in his body—the Church.

Think of prayer as a relationship. If you are in a relationship and you don't have any communication, then that relationship is not going to grow. I think of prayer, clearly, as being in the acknowledged presence of God. I am aware that I am only because God is, and that God has brought me into being, and that I depend totally, and utterly, on this God who loves me. And so, the thanks well up for all that God is, and God has done, and God will do. Prayer is not a single-layered thing. It is not one-way traffic. Through prayer you become, or try to become, or God makes you become, more and more like God.

JOHN POLKINGHORNE

About fifteen years ago, when I was a novice clergyman in Bristol, I had the experience of being suddenly, and quite unexpectedly, very seriously ill. I mean, it just came out of the blue. I had an abdominal problem, and I was whisked off to the hospital, to the emergency room. When I recovered from the operation, I was lying in my hospital bed, and my whole world was terrifically diminished. I was worn out, and my world had closed in, and I just sat there watching the drips that were keeping me alive. God seemed immensely far away. It was nearly impossible for me to pray, but I was very conscious of being prayed for by my family, by my church, and also by a community of Anglican nuns with whom I have a close connection. I felt myself inspired by the prayers of others at a time when I really wasn't able to pray much myself.

Twice, I actually had a sort of waking dream, or you might even call it a mild vision. I twice had this experience of suddenly seeing in my mind's eye one of the nuns praying for me. I visit the nuns at least once a year at their chapel. The sisters spend a great deal of time in prayer, and when you go to the chapel, there's very often a sister who is kneeling before the altar, motionless in prayer. And this picture came into my mind of the chapel at dusk, and the still figure of a sister praying for me. I thought they would be praying for God's wholeness and healing power for me, and this was very sustaining.

KATHLEEN NORRIS

When I am traveling, and very busy, and can't be with the monks or the sisters, just knowing that they are praying at different times of the day is an inspiration to me.

To ask someone to pray for us—a spiritual advisor, a friend—means that we confess to them our needs. Sometimes we confess not only our needs, but our failings. Our confessions can also be private—to

God alone. We confess because we want to be known, and to share what we ordinarily keep hidden—sometimes even hidden from ourselves. It is an act of freeing ourselves from secrets and lies, from behavior that we want to change. To confess is also to make a request. We ask God for help in correcting our mistakes. We ask Him to inspire us to change, and to forgive us.

This is the part of prayer that often makes people shy away from praying. It brings to mind that aspect of religion that is finger-wagging and rigid. *Confess—or else you will go to hell. Confess—or you will lose God's favor. Confess—change your ways. Confess—you are wrong. Confess—you're a sinner. Convert!*

To threaten someone into a confession is to miss the point. True confession comes when we are stirred inside to stop doing what we have been doing. Though we often tend to deny our failings, we are led to address them not through fear but through inspiration. We mirror the willing spirit of Psalm 38, "For I am ready to halt, and my sorrow is continually before me. For I will declare mine iniquity; I will be sorry for my sin" (17,18).

VISHWA MOHAN BHATT

Prayer for me is the means by which I can convey my feelings to God, and I believe it relieves me of the pain or anguish which swells in my heart at times. I pray when I am confused, and often this helps me to realize the mistakes I have made.

Just as we confess our mistakes, we also confess our faith. We confess our mistakes so that we might stop our mistakes. When we confess our faith, we make our faith stronger. By allowing our faith to be known, we allow ourselves to be known—what we believe, and what we love. What we love, we praise.

There are verses in Scripture that show that people praised God to the extreme. "I will praise thee with my whole heart: before the gods will I sing praise unto thee. I will worship toward thy holy temple, and praise thy name for thy loving kindness and for thy truth: for thou hast magnified thy word above all thy name. In the day when I cried thou answeredst me, and strengthenedst me with strength in my soul. All the kings of the earth shall praise thee, O Lord, when they hear the words of thy mouth. Yea, they shall sing in the ways of the Lord: for great is the glory of the Lord" (Psalm 138:1–5).

In this Psalm, David, the one who gives praise, is inspired to sing. He believes that God has answered his prayers, and he is filled with praise, poetry, and song. All of us have a tendency to point out what we praise, so that others might also praise it. When we see a good film, we tell people to go see it. When we read a good novel, we tell others about it. David believes that others are certain to share his praise for God, that they will also be singing.

David's song is one of joy. It is also a song of gratitude. Because our answers to prayer, our gifts, come by grace, we praise God because we are grateful.

DAVID CHECKETTS

Prayer is a yearning. It is the deepest emotions of the heart, the deepest feelings, the strongest needs. It is a deeply personal thing. A prayer can be said anywhere, at any time. I pray before I get into bed at night, and I pray before I leave my house in the morning. It is not a formal act, it is simply taking a moment to be grateful for what I have, for the health of my children, the love in my family, how blessed I have been. Gratitude is something I have tried to develop and never lose.

WYNTON MARSALIS

Giving thanks to God can come in any form. You don't have to get on your knees and give thanks. When I'm truly grateful for something I pray, and I pray when I don't have anything.

HELEN BAYLOR

The prayer that I pray the most is the prayer of thanksgiving. Sometimes I'll wake up in the morning and the first thing I'll say is "Thank you, Father." I'll begin to think about how I have been blessed, and I'll compare my life now to what it used to be fifteen, sixteen years ago, and all I can do is say, "Thank you, Father, I give you praise, I honor you, I glorify you, and I acknowledge that you are God." When I am seeking direction, I may just simply ask, "Father, is this something that you want for me to do? Is this the direction that you want me to take?" Prayer is simply just talking to God. I have never heard an audible voice with an answer to my prayers. But many times, I will get a *knowing* inside me. I then follow that by faith.

KATHERINE PATERSON

I read once that Bach wrote on all of his cantatas, *Soli Deo Gloria* ("to God alone, the glory"). So I write that on all my speeches, because I want to remember this when I'm speaking. Praying is a totally selfless act for me. So is writing. But when I speak, I'm very much thinking and talking about myself. And so, I want to remember that—the glory to God alone.

Our gratitude is not only expressed because our requests have been granted. God is praised in all circumstances—good and bad—as a confession of our faith. We praise in the spirit of Job, who said: "The Lord gave, and the Lord hath taken away; blessed be the name of the Lord" (Job 1:21).

Jack Polak, a Holocaust survivor, has experienced unspeakable personal tragedies, and has witnessed the depths of human indignities, but he still speaks about "the greatness of God." Polak is currently a successful investment counselor, and chairman emeritus of the Anne Frank Center, USA. Born in 1912 into a Jewish family living in Amsterdam, Polak's world was forever changed during World War II when the Nazis occupied the Netherlands. His parents were deported to the Sobibor death camp in the Lublin region of Poland, where they died in the gas chambers. Other family members died as well. Polak was sent to the concentration camp Bergen-Belsen in 1944. He was liberated by the Russian army in 1945, and emigrated to the United States in 1951.

JACK POLAK

There is a wonderful prayer, the *Shehecheyanu,* in which you say, "Thank you, God, that you have let me reach this day." It is a universal prayer; in every religion you will find something like it.

> *Blessed art thou, O Lord our God, King of the universe,*
> *who hast kept us in life, and hast preserved us, and*
> *enabled us to reach this season.*

Whenever I speak in a school, or in a church, or in a temple, when I end I will say, "Thank you, God, that you let me speak today." There have been many times, through prayer, that I have felt that the presence of God was close to me. One example would be when I was arrested in July 1942, just before deportation started. At that time, I was working as a CPA in an office, wearing my Jewish star, and suddenly the Germans came in, took all the Jews they could find, rounded us up, and marched us all through Amsterdam. Out of the four hundred people, they took ten and put them against the wall. I was one of the ten. Then ten German SS men came forward with their rifles drawn. At that moment, I said the Shema prayer, which is a prayer one says when you know you will die.

> *The Lord is King; the Lord was King;*
> *the Lord shall be King for ever and ever.*
> *Hear, O Israel: the Lord is our God, the Lord is One.*

I was not killed. They were shooting in the air. In some way, that incident gave me, in an instant, a tremendous amount of strength. At a much later date I was taken away in cattle cars from the concentration camp Bergen-Belsen to Troebitz, a town near Leipzig in eastern Germany—a train ride of two weeks. I had worked in the kitchen in Bergen-Belsen, which made me one of the stronger people. And because I was one of the stronger ones, every morning, when the train stopped, we were the ones who had to carry out the bodies of the ones who had died during the night. I still remember every one I had to dig a grave for. And I said the Kaddish, the Mourner's Prayer, while burying them. To this day, when I say the Kaddish prayer, I think about those times in Bergen-Belsen, and after I feel God's presence and a sense of peace.

Now, there are certain prayers which are difficult for me, particularly a prayer that is said on Rosh Hashanah, the Jewish New Year. This is a prayer in which we say that next year God will decide how somebody is going to die. One verse says you can die by the sword. Well, my brother-in-law was shot while fighting in the Resistance. Another says you can die by being stoned—my other brother-in-law was stoned to death in Mauthausen. You can die by burning—my father and mother died in the gas chambers of Sobibor. You can die by hunger—my sister died three days after the liberation, of hunger and typhus.

On the First Day of the year it is inscribed, and on the Fast Day of Atonement it is sealed and determined, how many shall pass by, and how many be born; who shall live, and who die; who shall finish his allotted time, and who not; who is to perish by fire, who by water, who by sword, and who by wild beasts; who by hunger, or who by thirst; who by an earthquake, or who by the plague; who by strangling or who by lapidation; who shall be at rest, and who shall be wandering; who to remain tranquil, and who to be disturbed; who shall reap enjoyment, and who be painfully afflicted; who grow rich, and who become poor; who shall be cast down, and who exalted. But Penitence, Prayer, and Charity, can avert the evil decree.

This prayer is so powerful and difficult because with every word I think about the people who died. How often has it happened in history that people in one family died that way? It happened in my time. But that's the greatness of God. Those prayers address things that are real.

Most prayers address what is real and reveal what is real about us. Our dialogue with God is intimate. To be inspired by God is intimate. Our spirit is being joined with His.

This is why our prayers often contain all aspects of prayer—petition, intercession, confession, and praise. The more texture we give to our supplications, the more intimate we are with God. The more inspired we are, the more texture we have—deeper layers of vision, focus, and achievement.

The Lord's Prayer includes each aspect of prayer:

> *Our Father which art in heaven,*
> *Hallowed be thy name.*
> *Thy kingdom come. Thy will be done*
> *in earth, as it is in heaven.*
> *Give us this day our daily bread.*
> *And forgive us our debts,*
> *as we forgive our debtors.*
> *And lead us not into temptation,*
> *but deliver us from evil:*
> *For thine is the kingdom, and the power, and the glory,*
> *for ever. Amen.*
>
> (MATTHEW 6:9–13)

When the disciples asked Jesus how to pray, this was Jesus' response: "When ye pray, say . . ." and then He taught them to say the Lord's Prayer. He did not say pray *only* the Lord's Prayer. It is more that He was referring to it as a model. It begins "Our Father," and asks that we come to God as a child would come to a parent. A father cares about his child, and listens to the child, and knows what the child needs. A father gives life to the child. It is a prayer to our Father, of petition, intercession, confession, and praise, and a prayer that asks for, and commits us to, forgiveness.

KATHLEEN NORRIS

The prayer that seems the most meaningful is the Lord's Prayer. It's the one in the Scriptures that Jesus gives us directly. It really offers everything that one needs in prayer.

TOBIAS WOLFF

I pray the Lord's Prayer every day. That is the one prayer that Scripture scholars seem to agree on as having Jesus' stamp on it, though I am not a Scripture scholar myself and I take a lot of that stuff with a grain of salt. But there is something about that prayer that has always spoken very powerfully to me, and it seems to say those things which need saying every day. It recognizes that we ourselves are not fountains of forgiveness, and helps us to be forgiving. It is a recognition of our familial relationship with God, and of ourselves as God's children. I think the central point about Jesus is his forgiveness. He didn't need to come down here and shake us all up, and kick us around, and scare us into being good. We already had Yahweh to do that. What Jesus is proposing is that we begin to forgive each other, to live less vengefully. But to be forgiven means you must forgive others. Jesus tells the parable about the landowner who calls up his servant who owes him money. The man says, I don't know what I can do, I can't pay you. Can you give me more time? And his master has mercy on him and forgives the debt. Then this guy goes out and grabs someone who owes him money and starts throttling him. That's the crucial moment. Having been forgiven, then we must do the same. It's the discipline that is most alien to human nature, it seems to me, and the one that most affects our life together, and that we have to learn again and again. That's one thing that speaks to me very powerfully in my reading of the Gospels, and in saying the Lord's Prayer.

Most of us who are reluctant to forgive are stuck in our reluctance. We really do not want to. When our hardness melts away, and we choose to forgive, what had once seemed like compromise and weakness now seems more in line with movement, growth, and love. Our vision and our actions have been changed. Inspiration is a breaking through of anything that is static, of anything that is without breath or movement—the dry spells in our work, the hardening of our hearts. It is what rouses us to see, and to act. It allows us to heal. And in healing, it breaks through whatever is static—our grief, our failings, our communication with others, our unwillingness to show compassion.

It is what opens us up, and opens our prayers. We pray most freely to God's Spirit when we are led by God's Spirit. We forget ourselves, and speak to Him in the way that we breathe—not continuously, like breathing, not every moment of the day, but without self-consciousness and without effort.

When I was a child, I always liked to see my breath in winter. It seemed like magic, that something invisible inside me would come out and look like smoke. I would stand outside with my friends, and we would show one another our breath. We would blow it back and forth between us. It would give us the most enormous childish joy—the breath, the freedom, the giving and receiving. Prayer, in its rawest sense, is the passing back and forth of breath—ours as it comes out with the words we send to God, and His breath, which keeps coming, that is always there.

RITUAL

LOVE, PATIENCE, FORGIVENESS, AND COMMUNITY

Whenever I'm on the Upper West Side, I go to Saint John the Divine, where there's a side altar for people who have died of AIDS, and to go there, buy a candle and light it, is so satisfying to me. There's something so grounding about that place and that experience, especially in all the external hustle and noise of New York City. I'm lighting this light which perhaps the dead could see, and which maybe God might see, and which is a visual form of memory. What I find compelling is that you are doing something that other people are also doing in a place that is set apart for it to be done. There is something terrifically powerful about formal actions in a sacred place.

MARK DOTY

STEVE REICH

I think that rituals, which are called mitzvoth commandments in Hebrew, will lead you to an understanding beyond what you would get by thinking about the complexities of matters of faith. I try to observe the dietary rules of my religion, and the Sabbath. I am by nature disposed toward working a lot and frequently, so it becomes significant that between the sundown on Friday and the sundown on Saturday, I stop composing, put on the phone machine, and spend time with my family. Sabbath is, for someone who is interested in meditation, like an extended period, and the more you can really observe it, which is to cleanse your mind of work, and to quench your discussion of work, then the more meditative you are. As for the dietary rules, a lot of people look at being kosher as archaic. Well, this commandment does come from an ancient text, but we have since learned that it is a pretty wise commandment because some of the foods that we don't eat aren't all that healthy. I have found that these commandments are something we have to accept as being in our best interests, and beyond our complete understanding. It is not just a question of faith, but of developed experience. I believe in God, but this is not why I follow rituals. Through the prayers and practices, you are led to something. This is what Judaism has taught me. First we do, then we understand.

Judaism is different than Christianity. In Christianity the focus is on what you believe, and whether or not you have faith in God. Jews, on the other hand, would say, "What do you do on Friday night? Light the candles, make a *Kiddush,* and maybe ten years from now you'll feel differently." It's a very behaviorist religion at the core, with a great deal of wisdom. What you do is what makes you feel, makes you know, and makes you believe. I think the idea in Christianity, as I understand it with my limited background, is that man has to strive upward to sort of be like God. You reach for God, and then you're free of this earth. The Judaic view seems diametrically opposed. It's like, if you could just get everything right here, God would finally come down, but you have to work so hard to pry him down.

I didn't embrace ritual initially. I was brought up as a Reformed Jew. I went to Hebrew school, but I learned nothing. And I got nothing. I had a bar mitzvah where I pointed at signs I could not read. I had transliterations that I had memorized. I was a dressed-up parrot. And all of this produced a rather negative reaction. Religion seemed to be uninteresting. In my search, I became a typical case— Jewish kid, knows nothing about Judaism, hostile to his own back-ground, finds solace in Eastern religion. I began to do hatha yoga regularly every morning, and I did the breathing exercises, which led to my doing some southern Buddhist meditation, and some northern Buddhist meditation, and some TM. All of which was really great, and yet it felt to me, at the time, that these were spiritual exercises, but that I was missing a religious core.

I met a lot of people in the sixties who were reading this Don Juan trilogy. And one of the things that Don Juan says in the book is that you have got to find your spot. I was thinking, Where's my spot? So I went to a bookstore and I got a book on kabbalah. I was carrying this book under my arm when I met my wife's parents for the first time. Her father noticed it and said, "How can you study kabbalah if you haven't studied Torah?" Now, I didn't know much, but I knew that was a good question. So I began studying biblical Hebrew, and the weekly portion of the Torah, and at the age of thirty-seven, I began to get the education that a kid who had any real background would get when he was five, six, seven, or eight. But my study of the Jewish religion and my participating in rituals made an enormous impact on my life.

Now, I know the word *religion* has become kind of a dirty word. People tend to use the word *spirituality,* because I think that what is running fairly deep among educated Jews and Christians is that there's something wrong with Judaism and there's something wrong with Christianity. People tend to think that anybody who is really devoted to either one of them is some kind of fanatic, or fundamentalist, or idiot. Whereas people think if you're "spiritual" this means that you don't know exactly what it is you believe, but you feel these rumblings. Well, everybody feels these rumblings, but I believe that through the doing, through the ritual, we go beyond the rumblings to understanding.

The rumblings inside us tell us things. They tell us that we are thirsty, hungry, angry, or in love. They tell us that we are wanting something that we do not have at hand—or at least do not have in our hands right then. When our rumblings tell us that we are hungry for God, we feel stirred inside, inspired to search, yet we often do not know where to start. We might take a step toward our religion, or toward a different religion, or we might not move at all, fearing that religion will bore us or quickly kill our rumblings, that it will offer only judgment, not inspiration.

Often we are more resistant to those who are "religious" than to religion, to those who lead people with fear or try to convert. Inspiration leads us with love, not fear. And we go forward seeking more than communion with people. We come rumbling for more than bread and wine. We come inspired by God, in search of God, and sometimes we seek Him through symbols.

The candle, bread, and wine are part of the Sabbath. Observing the Sabbath reminds those who participate in this ritual that God rested on the seventh day of Creation, that He rested after He worked, and that one specific night of the week is to be set aside, after work, for rest and for nourishment. "Remember the sabbath day, to keep it holy. Six days shalt thou labour, and do all thy work: But the seventh day is the sabbath of the Lord thy God; in it thou shalt not do any work. . . . For in six days the Lord made heaven and earth, the sea, and all that in them is, and rested the seventh day: wherefore the Lord blessed the Sabbath day, and hallowed it" (Exodus 20:8–11).

In any ritual, the bread, the wine, the candles we light are only sacred if they are sacred to us. Bread and wine help us to remember the Sabbath or the Last Supper, or they are simply food and drink. A candle is lit to remember the dead, or it is lit for mood and light.

Many of us are stirred by the symbol of light. There is something mystical about the candles we light for the dead, or for Sabbath, or Advent. Or the candles we light on our birthdays. Light, in various ways, is a symbol for life. Our world was brought to life with breath and light. When "the earth was without form, and void; and darkness was upon the face of the deep. And the Spirit of God moved upon the face of the waters," God said His first words: "Let there be light" (Genesis 1:2–3). With light there can be form and life. With light we see our life.

To inspire is to en*light*en. We are filled with clearer vision. We see. We become empowered because we see. God makes man's spirit "enlightened with the light of the living" (Job 33:30).

Desmond Tutu uses the image of fire when speaking about God's Spirit.

DESMOND TUTU

When you are in the presence of the Holy Spirit, it is like sitting in front of a fire that does not burn you, but suffuses you with its qualities—its warmth, glow, and color. And as you are there, in the presence of the Spirit, you also become suffused with the divine attributes of compassion, gentleness, and love, without your doing anything about it except to be there. You are loved, and you are held in this love.

In the early days, when I was still young, I was being trained in techniques of prayer. I engaged in meditation, and there was a great deal of activity on my part. But as I have grown older, and have learned from others more experienced in the ways of the Spirit, I have become more and more aware that the activity is first initiated by God. In Psalm 81, the Lord, speaking through the psalmist, says, "Open wide your mouth, and I will fill it" (NIV).

This is not to say that we cannot cultivate attitudes and practices that make it easier for the Spirit to inspire us. Because we are the incarnation of body and spirit, we would not be able to survive on that which is only spirit. And it is a mercy to know that the sacramental grace of God, for us in the Anglican Church, is available to us through physical things—through the bread and the wine, through the laying on of hands. It does not depend on how I feel when it comes to rituals. There are many times in life when we go through periods of desolation, when we get a sense that God is removed, that He is not really present. But it is important that we have discipline, despite our feelings. It is important to know that we have set aside time—maybe in the morning, at midday, or in the evening—for these physical things, these tangible things, these ordinary things which are sanctified. All of these have the capacity to communicate the divine life.

Andre Dubus also brought up this issue of doing rituals, not out of feeling, but out of faith.

ANDRE DUBUS

The Eucharist is very important to me. It always has been. For me it is the actual body and blood of Christ. I mean, I really believe that I'm having some physical contact with God, so I need that. Religious rituals bring me closer to God, but I can't get broad and assume that they do this for other people. I'm more in harmony if I'm taking part in them. A friend of mine, who is a recovering alcoholic, said her sponsor told her that it doesn't matter how you feel, just put your body at the meeting. I thought, Boy, that's good advice. That's good. I need that. I'm incapable of meditation and contemplation. My mind is everywhere. My mind is everywhere in Mass. It's all over the place, which has made me absolutely distrust the human mind. So I understand when her sponsor says it doesn't matter how you feel, just put your body at the meeting. Usually when the body gets there, you get there with it.

William James says, in one of his essays—he's actually quoting a book by a woman in the nineteenth century—that if you don't have faith, just act like you have it anyway. You have to act the way you want to feel. I would say to a person—pray. Whether you feel it or not. Who cares about feelings? My last wife was absolutely surprised when I told her I was getting up to go to daily Mass and I didn't feel like going. She said, "Then why are you going?" I said, "It has nothing to do with feeling. I go because I know it's a good thing." Two or three minutes after receiving Communion, I feel some kind of harmony and peace.

⊠

Part of our motivation for performing any ritual is that we can imagine what might happen if we didn't. Waking up and showering, getting our mail, getting coffee at almost the same time from the same place each day are not always things we come to with speed. Our feet almost move us mechanically. We do not wake up saying, "I want to be productive, clean, informed, alert," and yet the thought of the consequences and chaos of not being these things is enough to put us in motion. We cannot always wait to *want* to do something before we act. Often we find that we want to do it only *as* we do it.

This is also true of inspiration. It often comes *during* what we do, not before. Rituals like showering and getting mail are not the same as the sacraments, or the rituals of any religion. But they are comparable in this regard: by doing them we shape our days and, ultimately, our lives. And that is the comfort of all rituals. They ground, expand, and stir us. They make us who we are. On some level, we become them.

Sometimes we participate in a ritual so that we might learn the ritual. We go through the motions so that we might understand. During our conversation with Mark Richard, the author of *Fishboy* (a novel) and of two short story collections, *Charity,* and *The Ice at the Bottom of the World,* he said, "I can honestly say that sometimes I have participated in rituals when I have felt very far from God, when I felt as if I were just going through the motions. I was trying to find God, and find my way. Walker Percy said it best. He said we come here, and we're trying to find our way, and that is the burden of Catholics, that we come into the world already saddled with sin and guilt and we're trying to find a way out of it and redeem ourselves. That interests me as a writer. Even if I weren't a Christian that would interest me."

Richard said he felt a step closer to "finding his way" after he encouraged his friend, the author Jennifer Allen, to get baptized. After he accompanied Allen to confirmation classes and to the baptism ceremony, he wound up becoming her godfather and, eventually, her husband.

MARK RICHARD

Jennifer had been a friend of mine in New York for years and years. She was living in California when I went out to do an article on Tom Waits for *Spin* magazine, and I stayed at her house. I was only supposed to be in California for one night, but I ended up spending close to three weeks out there. While I was there, I noticed that Jennifer would go to services at the Catholic church in Santa Monica, and that she would burn devotional candles from the church, and pray. I asked her about her faith and I found out that she had never been baptized. Her mother had had bad experiences with a Catholic priest before and said that she was going to let her children decide for themselves what their religious orientation would be. After I left California, I eventually went to Tennessee to be the Tennessee Williams fellow at Sewanee, University of the South, which is one of the largest Episcopal seminaries in the country, and Jennifer came up to visit. I thought that it was important for her to be baptized and I kept saying, "It's nice for you to burn candles, but if you really don't understand, it's not going to yield for you." I just felt that if she was going to go that far, she might go a little farther. So she decided to take confirmation classes at Sewanee, but she felt a little uncomfortable going by herself, so I said that I would go, and that I would be reaffirmed. We went to all the classes together, and we learned about how the Episcopal Church broke off from the Catholic Church, the whole history, the rites, the rituals, what they mean, the holidays, everything. Eventually we found out that before Jennifer could get baptized, she would need a sponsor, someone who would present her. I said that I would present her.

During the ceremony, Jennifer was nervous. She was holding a candle while she was being baptized, and she caught The Book of Common Prayer on fire. But it turned out to be a beautiful ceremony, and very moving.

About two weeks later we received a package from the archdiocese. It said, "This is to certify Mark James Richard, godfather of Jennifer Diane Allen, godchild." We were both standing in the kitchen looking at this, and Jennifer said, "Oh my God! You're my godfather?"

As her godfather, I'm entrusted with her spiritual walk. If she has questions of faith, I'm the person that she is supposed to ask. Over time, as I have answered her questions, I have had to reexamine my own faith. She still has questions, and so do I, but I don't believe in blind faith. I think it is good to search for answers.

This whole experience with Jennifer has put me on a path that I had not followed with any other person that I had been involved with. There is a spiritual element in the relationship that I never had before. And the way the relationship moved, engagement became a logical step. Marriage became a logical step. Having a child became a logical step. They say that in a marriage you have three partners—the husband, the wife, and the third partner is God. So even when the communication breaks down between the husband and wife, there is still that connection between them through God. The fact that I thought a friend of mine should be baptized has brought me into a very good, productive marriage, and because of this event, because of God, I find myself changing in many ways.

When we look back at the changes in our lives that we believe we were led to by God, it is hard to tell what played more of a part— something we did, or our intentions behind what we did. Did it have to do with our attitude, faith, or motive, or was it our action? The same question could be asked about the benefits of ritual. Is ritual effective because of the intentions of the one doing it, or because of the ritual itself?

For every person we see yawning in churches and temples, we also see the bright-eyed or teary-eyed person who the service has moved. When we feel inclined to follow a tradition that honors God, no matter what brought us there, what our motive was, or how much we yawn, we have chosen to *follow,* which means something has led us. We could have chosen to be anywhere else, but we are there. To come without faith *is* faith. When we move toward the divine, we change. When we move without a sound motive, we still change. Our motives and attitudes are not to be ignored, but they matter less than our actions.

People are drawn to rituals in ways that they cannot even explain. The poet Kathleen Norris, who had a Protestant background, found herself drawn to the rituals and community at a Benedictine monastery, and this led her to become a Benedictine oblate. In her book about this experience, *The Cloister Walk,* Norris wrote: "When I became a Benedictine oblate, I knew two things: I didn't feel ready to do it, but I had to act, to take the plunge. I also had no idea where it would lead."[1] Norris talks about the sense of being led and inspired to keep coming back to this community, and about how daily rituals can bring daily revelations.

KATHLEEN NORRIS

I was raised to think of ritual as something dead in the past, not relevant to modern people. But I have found that gathering together with other people to do very traditional Christian things like daily

Bible reading and daily prayer has great meaning for me. My becoming a Benedictine oblate was really by divine accident, my stumbling around in the dark and finding these people in the middle of North Dakota, where everyone thinks that nothing ever happens. Well, that's where I ran into the Benedictines. I had gone up to this monastery to hear Carol Bly, a Minnesota writer, give a reading, and that was it. I just wanted to keep coming back, and I didn't know why. I had a generic Protestant upbringing, and I really didn't know much about the Catholic Church, the Catholic tradition, any of that. I was really incredibly ignorant, but I just kept going back because I liked their prayer life. I liked the people. On faith, I believed that I was being led to something, but it took me years to really figure out what.

I kept going back, without fully understanding. Finally, someone eventually suggested that I become a Benedictine oblate, which means an associate of a monastery. You attach yourself to a particular monastery, and as much as possible, as much as your life allows you to, you live by the Rule of Saint Benedict, which stresses love, patience, forgiveness, and community. Almost every monastery I can think of has quite a few associates, people who just sort of fall in love with this community and want it to be more a part of their lives. For me, it was my first experience of being with a community of people who were willing to gather for morning, noon, and evening prayer on a daily basis, and to have a daily Bible reading. What particularly appealed to me was that there had been people in the Christian tradition doing this for seventeen hundred years. That sense of continuity and tradition is very inspiring.

One of the greatest joys for me of Benedictine life is to be exposed to so much of the Scripture, and to find out what a source of inspiration the Bible really is. There's just about everything in there. Horrifying things. Glorious things. Sad things. No matter what is going on in my life, I can find something in the Bible that addresses that particular situation. The Benedictines also practice something called *lectio,* the spiritual reading that Benedictines want all monastic people to do. You do a slow, meditative reading, primarily of Scripture. The Benedictines read through whole books of the Bible in their prayer life, and they read it aloud. You're listening to entire books of the Bible, and as you sit there, listening, you become receptive to the words and inspired by them. When you hear the words read aloud, they enter the body in a funny way. The words enter your consciousness in a different way than if you were reading the Bible intellectually. You become still, open, immersed in Scripture, and the words really sink in. From the daily practices of prayer and *lectio* come daily revelations. And I think this has helped me to see faith and religion in terms of daily life, not something that's reserved for special times and special places. If it's a living faith, it's going to keep coming up in the course of ordinary living.

When we are inspired, though we may seem to be moving along effortlessly, it is usually our effort that has brought us to this point. Through consistent practice of our work or faith we do more, see more, open up more, and often receive more. Sacraments are rituals that Catholics and Protestants do in order to become more intimate with Christ, more open to receiving His grace.

The sacrament of Holy Communion is about communion and forgiveness—communion with Jesus, who died so that there would be the forgiveness of sin, and communion among Christians with one another. The bread and wine that are served represent the body and blood of Christ—literally or symbolically. For Protestants, the bread and wine are symbols. For Catholics, they are the actual body and blood of Christ, honoring the verses in Scripture that say "For my flesh is meat indeed, and my blood is drink indeed. He that eateth my flesh, and drinketh my blood, dwelleth in me, and I in him" (John 6:55,56). But either way, as body or symbol, the image we are left with is of God being absorbed into us and filling us—the most visual image of inspiration.

Religious rituals are often woven into everyday life, and can be as regular and automatic as waking, showering, getting coffee or mail. To wake up and pray, or read Scripture, or to go to daily Mass, to make this as routine as any of our secular routines, creates a rhythm and an opening in our lives. The regularity of doing these things reinforces the spiritual message behind the words and acts.

Hakeem Olajuwon has made daily rituals a priority in his life. As a devout Muslim, Olajuwon studies the Qur'an every day. The Qur'an is composed of the sacred writings that are accepted by Muslims as revelations made to the Prophet Muhammad by God (Allah) through the angel Gabriel. "As a Muslim," Olajuwon said, "we look at everything from the light of the Qur'an, and the Prophet's teaching." Central to these teachings are various rituals and acts of worship, referred to as the Five Pillars of Islam. These include: (1) the declaration of the belief in the sole deity of Allah, and in Muhammad as his prophet; (2) the practice of praying five times a day; (3) fasting during the month of Ramadan, the ninth month of the Islamic year; (4) helping the poor by giving from one's assets; and (5) participating in the hajj, the pilgrimage to Mecca, the birthplace of Islam.

HAKEEM OLAJUWON

Islam is all about practice. When you do certain rituals, like praying and fasting, the result is that you have peace. Muslims pray five times a day. The first prayer is before sunrise. The second one is the noon prayer. The third is in the afternoon. The fourth one is the sunset prayer. And the last one is at 8:00 P.M. before going to sleep. You can go to any country, and for any of the five prayer times, it will be the same prayers for those particular times. The purpose of the five daily prayers is that each prayer purifies you for the next prayer, and for the next prayer, and for the next. We pray and we fast in order to feel closer to God, which is the highest reward. People may think of fasting as difficult, but it is like a training program. It trains you to have self-discipline, and this will change the way in which you approach life. Everything that I do is directed by my duty to God. During the month of Ramadan, when I fast, my basketball statistics actually go much higher.

Every year I go to Mecca for umrah, to pray and to purify myself. About one million people attend. When I go there during hajj, there are three million people from all over the world, people from all ethnic backgrounds praying and expressing their gratitude to God. You see people everywhere, and their heads move like waves. You cannot see the end to them. Once you reach the level of purification that you reach at hajj, you change. You have changed your state of consciousness because your first priority from then on is to do the will of God.

Hearing the recitation of the Qur'an is another inspiring aspect of my faith. It touches my heart. I feel it. I tremble. It is the wealth of knowledge and the enlightenment that I get from it which is the inspiration.

Just as Hakeem Olajuwon feels that the pilgrimage to Mecca has changed him, Brazilian author Paulo Coelho said that he had a turning point in his life after taking a pilgrimage to Santiago. Coelho has published *The Alchemist, The Pilgrimage, By the River Piedra I Sat Down and Wept,* and *The Fifth Mountain.*

PAULO COELHO

The road to Santiago is a very ancient road that is one of the three sacred roads of Christianity. The first road led to the tomb of Saint Peter in Rome. The second led to the holy sepulcher of Christ in Jerusalem. And the third, the road to Santiago, led to the remains of the apostle Saint James. They say that in the beginning of Christianity, Saint James went to Spain to preach the Gospel, and when he returned to Jerusalem he was killed. Somebody took his body to Spain and buried him in a place where, years later, a shepherd saw falling stars. Then the shepherd discovered his body. This place is now called Santiago de Compostela. *Santiago* is for "Saint James," and *de Compostela,* the "field of stars." Eventually there began pilgrimages to this place where Saint James is supposedly buried. Today we are able to follow a map that a monk drew at the end of the ninth century. You can go by foot or by bicycle. There is an energy on that road, and through that energy I felt the presence of God. This was a turning point for me. Before this, I had been searching. Though I had grown up Catholic, I was searching for a spiritual path. I tried a bit of everything, including the rituals of Buddhism and Hinduism. I was trying to choose every road, but I had no focus and, therefore, no connection. Following the road to Santiago taught me that we cannot travel every single road; we have to choose one that leads us to God. By following the spiritual journey, the journey started to guide me. Once I decided to walk, something changed in me. When I allow myself to experience the breath of God, I experience revelation.

Coelho's pilgrimage is in keeping with the tradition of those who have followed the same path for centuries before him. Olajuwon's annual pilgrimage, which is also in keeping with the tradition of millions who journey to the birthplace of Islam, involves worshiping with others. When we worship with others, we form a community. As a community, our experience is singular, and also the same. The difference between worshiping by ourselves or with others is like the difference between listening to a symphony by ourselves, in our home, or hearing it at a concert. Alone, we can still sense the Spirit in the work, the mastery and the passion, but hearing it with others, live, and in the moment, adds another dimension. We are all present for the same event, even if we are not moved to the same degree. We are a roomful of life, of heartbeats and breath, and for that moment, for that experience, there is an all-sided exchange—the Spirit in the work filling our spirits, and the Spirit that we receive hovering between us.

In a religious community we are bound together by that Spirit hovering between us. Despite our differences we are linked by this Spirit, the way blood links each member of a family.

KATHERINE PATERSON

I think the communal aspect of worship is very important for us. We're not solitary creatures. In the Christian imagery, we're all together. We're the body of Christ—not one of us, but all together—and we need each other. We're different, and we're meant to be different, and we're meant to be together.

R E V E R E N D
J E A N - P I E R R E   R U I Z

As a priest, it is my privilege to preside at the Eucharist, and I have the good fortune of living in a parish community, and in a rectory, where I am able to celebrate the Eucharist with people in whose neighborhood I live. The fact that this community can gather together day in, day out, week in, week out, during the different seasons of the year, with the different experiences of their lives and bring that to the celebration of the Eucharist is, for me, as a presider and a preacher, very edifying. The sacramental life, the Eucharistic life of the Church means that, to some extent, my entire life is lived according to those rhythms. One is never outside the Church, so to speak. And I experience that as a nurturing and a challenging fact. Living this way moves me beyond myself, and moves me to action and reflection.

D I A N A   E C K

I think that the ritual and sustenance of a religious community are extremely important. I am a member of a church and I go as often as I can. I don't always make it every Sunday because I'm sometimes away on the weekends. But I believe that the sustenance of faith in the context of a community, a community of prayer and of song and of celebration, is extremely important. It is also important in structuring one's sense of time, through the seasons and through the liturgical year. I think about the year in terms of its liturgical seasons. I would not miss going to church the first Sunday in Advent and throughout that season, and through the Christmas and Epiphany seasons, and on into Lent, and then through the season of Easter and Pentecost. These are all very important moments in the life of the community. I feel that there's a sense in which ritual sustains us and holds us, especially when we experience tragedy, illness, death, or times of deep loneliness or despair. At these times, even "going through the motions" of ritual often enables us to move forward, and to reclaim our orientation. Ritual is important both for the life of the community, and also for the life of the individual.

Anything can become our community. Our church or temple, our place of work. In the children's wing of many hospitals, some of the staff sing Christmas and Hanukkah songs for—and with—the children each season. A group of dancers I know, before each performance, forms a circle, holds hands, and prays. Film director Ang Lee talks about how he compares the ritual that he does with his cast and crew before shooting his films to a prayer.

ANG LEE

I do an opening ceremony before each movie, a Chinese ceremony, with the whole cast and crew. Before we begin filming, we put a sacrifice—a ham or a chicken—on a table and pray. There is also fruit, bread, and three types of liquid—wine, tea, and water. I give everyone incense, and I take a reed, bow it to the four directions, and end up facing south. On the table is a big bowl of rice so people can stick their incense into it after we pray. Then before I hit the gong, a cinematographer will run the camera a little bit to symbolize that we are beginning to shoot the film. Many Chinese filmmakers do this ceremony, and people really seem to respond well to it. It's like a prayer. I learned from Christian prayers that you shouldn't pray in order to gain something. You should pray to have the strength to be able to take whatever comes. I say to everybody, "Just be calm for a little while," and we all become silent. I think this ceremony is very good for putting ourselves aside, and for allowing inspiration to fill us. When you push your burdens aside, when you pray, things work out. You become open for things to work out.

Rick Moody wrote *The Ice Storm,* on which the movie, directed by Ang Lee, was based. He attended Lee's ceremony, and noted a similarity between this ritual and his own ritual of praying before he works. The purpose of both rituals is to ask God for inspiration.

RICK MOODY

James Shamus, the producer of *The Ice Storm,* called me and said, "On the first day of shooting, Ang does this Buddhist ceremony, and everyone is going to be there. You've got to be there, too. It's really fun, so come on out." So I drove with James to New Canaan, Connecticut, where they were filming *The Ice Storm.* The first day of filming happened to be in this park where I used to play Little League soccer, so it was very strange.

Before this ceremony, I had been approaching this film as I had approached the book—as a very Western experience. The book is about a family from the Connecticut suburbs. It's a very American story. But Ang brings Eastern ways of thinking and ways of faith to his work, and therefore brings a really interesting cross-cultural current to stories that are less Eastern and more Western in their intent.

The whole cast was at the opening ceremony, including Kevin Kline, Sigourney Weaver, Joan Allen, Christina Ricci, Elijah Wood, and some child actors. I think everyone was feeling a sort of giddy awe, and moved by the idea of invoking God, or whatever the Buddhist equivalent is, at the beginning of a creative endeavor. When I wrote *The Ice Storm,* I prayed every day before going to work. I often felt that I was not good enough to accomplish what I wanted to accomplish, and so I prayed that God would help me, and show me His way. I was moved by the fact that Ang invoked his faith before he began filming *The Ice Storm,* in the same way that I invoked my faith when I tried to write the book.

To ask God to help us is to ask Him to move toward us. As distant as God seems at times, He is never closer than when we are inspired—as close as the blood pumping through us, as close as our breath. God as an idea does not inspire us. God who is "out there," or maybe not out there, who does not breathe life into us through our prayers and invocations, whose grace and Spirit are not whirling inside us, but just words, this God does not inspire us. Only God living through us, working through us, only through touch does God inspire.

During our conversation with Reverend Jean-Pierre Ruiz, he said, "The church's sacramental ritual, the Mass in particular, is central and vital to nourishing my own relationship with God. It is a point of contact with God, and because of the form that it takes, it is also a point of contact with other human beings."

Inspiration is that point of contact. It is not one party's experience alone. For one to contact another, both have to be there.

REVEREND
JEAN-PIERRE RUIZ

I find that today's culture is a culture that is profoundly in search of meaningful symbols. Not easy answers, but tangible signs of a purposeful and challenging and loving, personal God who becomes involved with human beings, and who speaks to human beings in terms that human beings can understand, and to which human beings can respond. I think that is the dynamic of the incarnation, in that God not only shared life with us, by virtue of God's creating us, but that God shared life with us by becoming one of us in the person of Jesus. I find that compelling, I find that energizing, I find that a tremendous sign of hope for people who may think that God seems fairly distant.

In the Hispanic community, there are often economic disadvantages, and challenges of many kinds. Many Latinos arrive in the United States as a result of economic disadvantages experienced in their nations of origin, and poverty often persists for them while they are in the United States. For this community, there is a great identification with the suffering of Jesus, and a recognition that God is involved with—and God is concerned about—the suffering and deprivation that the people experience in a very, very real way. There is an identification with a God who is not distant, but a crucified God who bleeds with the wounds of the people.

A God who bleeds with our wounds is a God of compassion. At that point of contact between God's Spirit and ours, the Spirit of compassion passes through our spirit. We open our hearts, we love, we forgive. We need inspiration for our hearts as much as for our work.

Inspiration heightens our compassion the way that it heightens our vision.

Jack Polak saw a moment of this divine compassion, on Yom Kippur (the Day of Atonement), while he was a prisoner in a concentration camp.

JACK POLAK

One of the most unbelievable events in my life occurred in 1944. I was working in the kitchen in Bergen-Belsen on Yom Kippur. I had started at three o'clock in the morning, and had worked until eight o'clock in the evening. Of course I got food—that was the good part of the job—but it was unbelievably hard work. I decided not to fast that day. At three o'clock in the afternoon we were working hard. Suddenly, the *Oberscharfuehrer,* the man who was in charge of the kitchen, a rotten man who was hanged after the war, came forward and said in German, "Who is fasting?" We didn't even know that he knew it was a Jewish holiday. Three young men came forward, and one of them said, "We are fasting." We didn't know what the man was going to do. Was he going to hit them or kill them or God knows what? But he said, "Here is wurst, and here is bread, and here is butter. Take it. I want you to go to your barrack and pray." What must have gone on in his mind? Maybe he was a good Christian in his young years. Maybe God spoke to his heart and moved him to act that way. Here you have a sense of divine intervention in the middle of the most unbelievable horror. After that, we finished the Yom Kippur in silence.

Whether or not God is present or intervenes in our lives is not something you can prove. I am a very practical man. I want to talk about things that can be proven. However, when you are a witness to what happened on Yom Kippur in Bergen-Belsen, you find out that God's presence has nothing to do with anything practical.

Being open to the possibility that God does watch over us, that he does intervene in our lives, can only make life easier for people, and this was true in the concentration camps. It seemed to me that people who had faith died more peaceful deaths than those who did not. Those of us in the camps who put our faith in God felt that we had something to live for.

My wife and I started a relationship just before we were taken to the camps. We kept our relationship going in the camps by writing each other letters. I have 120 letters that we wrote to each other in our native language, Dutch, and that have since been translated into English. In many of those letters, we talk about our sense of God's presence in the midst of the worst of times, and this inspired us to keep going.

Right after the war, though I did not feel particularly religious, I went to the synagogue on the high holidays. I was standing all the way in the back when somebody came over to me and said, "Mr. Polak, will you please come forward. I want you to stand in the first row." I looked around in that synagogue, and there was nobody I knew. Then the full impact of what had happened during the war really, truly hit me. At that time I was thirty-two years old, and I was standing in a row where normally only the elders who had been serving the Jewish community for years stand. And there I was. At that moment, I felt the need to try, in whatever small way, to make up for the six million who were not as lucky as I to survive. And that is what I have been doing. When the *Los Angeles Times* once interviewed me, someone asked, "What is your goal in life?" And I told them that it is to bring Jews and non-Jews together so that a thing like the Holocaust cannot happen again. I thank God that I survived, and I feel that it must be God who is inspiring me to serve not just the Jewish community, but every community.

✶

What do we serve without inspiration? What do we see without divine sight? How much life is in our life without the breath of life?

Inspiration puts us on a mission. We want to serve—our work, our community, our God. We serve in the heightened state of energy and life that pushes past the normal barriers. Fear does not stop us for we are able to see past fear. Time does not stop us, for we feel immortal and fully alive. We trust that time will open for us, for our mission. We are too filled to feel empty, too stirred to feel tired. We are too loved to feel alone.

Luke Ripley, the narrator of Andre Dubus's short story "A Father's Story," is a man who lives by rituals. He goes to bed early, wakes at four forty-five, and has an hour of silence. He makes his bed, drinks coffee, and smokes. Daily, he prays, goes to Mass, and receives the Eucharist. "I have learned . . . the necessity and wonder of ritual," he says. "For ritual allows those who cannot will themselves out of the secular to perform the spiritual, as dancing allows the tongue-tied man a ceremony of love."[2]

Luke Ripley, a man who is so tied to his religious tradition that he will not even allow himself to remarry, does not report a hit-and-run car accident that his daughter is responsible for, to protect her from the police, knowing that the boy his daughter left lying by the road will die.

This is a father's story. It is about love so strong that we come to our child's rescue at all costs. It is about being on a mission to save someone, to revive someone, to love. It is about unconditional, intimate love. Though the choices made to do this were human and not divine—there is nothing divine about neglecting the dying boy—this father's ferocious love describes God's love. It is not a love we earn, but a love we receive. It is a life-giving love, a healing love, a love that instantly or gradually changes us. When we receive this love, we are like the psalmist, filled with new vision, new life, and songs, and our mission is to sing them.

NOTES

PROLOGUE

[1] Sally Fitzgerald, ed., *The Habit of Being: Letters of Flannery O'Connor* (New York: Farrar, Strauss and Giroux, 1979), p. 387.

[2] Patrick Kavanaugh, *The Spiritual Lives of Great Composers* (Nashville: Sparrow Press, 1992), p. 77.

[3] Madeleine L'Engle, *Walking on Water: Reflections on Faith and Art* (Wheaton, Illinois: Harold Shaw Publishers, 1980), p. 149.

THE BREATH OF GOD

[1] Kathleen Norris, *The Cloister Walk* (New York: Riverhead Books, 1996), p. 331.

[2] Agnes Sanford, *The Healing Light* (New York: Ballantine Books, 1983), p. 62.

[3] Mary Kittredge, *The Encyclopedia of Health: The Respiratory System* (New York: Chelsea House Publishers, 1989), p. 18.

LOSS, GRIEF, AND HEALING: WHERE IS GOD?

[1] Andre Dubus, *Broken Vessels* (Boston: David R. Godine, 1994), p. 194.

[2] Andre Dubus, *Selected Stories* (New York: Vintage Books, 1989), p. 458.

[3] Mark Doty, *Heaven's Coast* (New York: HarperCollins Publishers, 1996), p. 299.

REVELATION: BEFORE AND AFTER

[1] Frederick Buechner, *The Magnificent Defeat* (San Francisco: HarperSan-Francisco, 1985), p. 99.

[2] Charles T. Dougherty, "Did Paul Fall Off a Horse?" *Bible Review,* vol. XIII, no. 4 (August 1997), pp. 43–44.

[3] William James, *Varieties of Religious Experience* (New York: Penguin Books, 1985), p. 185.

[4] These words, written by Christopher Parkening, appeared in the liner notes to his album *Simple Gifts,* Angel Records, 1992.

[5] Frederick Buechner, *The Magnificent Defeat,* pp. 119–20.

[6] Reverend Joan Brown Campbell is quoted as saying this in David Herszenhorn's article, which appeared in *The New York Times,* February 28, 1997.

CREATIVITY

[1] Madeleine L'Engle, *Walking on Water,* p. 81.

[2] Patrick Kavanaugh, *The Spiritual Lives of Great Composers,* p. 95.

[3] Thomas Merton, *The Ascent to Truth* (New York: Harcourt Brace Jovanovich, 1979), p. 184.

[4] These words from William Faulkner's interview with Jean Stein were taken from *Writers at Work: The Paris Review Interviews,* ed. Malcolm Cowley (New York: The Viking Press, 1959), p. 134.

PRAYER: IN DIALOGUE WITH GOD

[1] Frederick Buechner, *The Magnificent Defeat,* pp. 125–26.

[2] William James, *Varieties of Religious Experience,* p. 464.

[3] Thomas Merton, *Thoughts in Solitude* (New York: Farrar, Strauss and Giroux, 1988), p. 53.

RITUAL: LOVE, PATIENCE, FORGIVENESS, AND COMMUNITY

[1] Kathleen Norris, *The Cloister Walk,* p. xi.

[2] Andre Dubus, *Selected Stories,* pp. 460–61.

PERMISSIONS

PROLOGUE

[1] *The Habit of Being: Letters of Flannery O'Connor,* ed. Sally Fitzgerald. Copyright © 1979 by Regina O'Connor. Reprinted by permission of Farrar, Strauss and Giroux, Inc.

[2] *The Spiritual Lives of Great Composers* by Patrick Kavanaugh, copyright © 1992. Used by permission of Sparrow Press/EMI Christian Music Publishing.

[3] *Walking on Water: Reflections on Faith and Art* by Madeleine L'Engle. Copyright © 1980. Used by permission of Harold Shaw Publishers, Wheaton, IL 60189.

THE BREATH OF GOD

[1] Reprinted by permission of Riverhead Books, a division of the Putnam Publishing Group, from *The Cloister Walk* by Kathleen Norris. Copyright © 1996 by Kathleen Norris.

[2] Reprinted by permission of Macalester Park Publishing Company from *The Healing Light* by Agnes Sanford. Copyright © 1947 by Macalester Park Publishing Company.

[3] Reprinted by permission of Chelsea House Publishers, Philadelphia, from *The Encyclopedia of Health: The Respiratory System* by Mary Kittredge. Copyright © 1989 by Mary Kittredge.

Interviews, ed. Malcolm Cowley. Copyright © 1958 by The Paris Review, Inc.

PRAYER: IN DIALOGUE WITH GOD

[1] Reprinted by permission of HarperCollins Publishers, Inc. *The Magnificent Defeat* by Frederick Buechner. Copyright © 1966 by Frederick Buechner. Copyright renewed 1994 by Frederick Buechner.

[2] Reprinted by permission of Penguin Books from *Varieties of Religious Experience* by William James. First published in the U.S. in 1902. Published in The Penguin American Library, 1982.

[3] Excerpt from *Thoughts in Solitude* by Thomas Merton, Copyright © 1958 by the Abbey of Our Lady of Gethsemani. Copyright renewed © 1986 by the Trustees of the Thomas Merton Legacy Trust. Reprinted by permission of Farrar, Straus and Giroux, Inc.

RITUAL: LOVE, PATIENCE, FORGIVENESS, AND COMMUNITY

[1] Reprinted by permission of Riverhead Books, a division of the Putnam Publishing Group from *The Cloister Walk* by Kathleen Norris. Copyright © 1996 by Kathleen Norris.

[2] Reprinted by permission of Vintage Books, a division of Random House, Inc., New York. *Selected Stories* by Andre Dubus. Copyright © 1989 by Andre Dubus.

NOTE REGARDING BIBLE TRANSLATIONS

All Scripture quotations marked (NIV) are taken from the Holy Bible, New International Version®. NIV®. Copyright © 1973, 1978, 1984 by International Bible Society. Used by permission of Zondervan Publishing House. All rights reserved.

All Scripture quotations marked (NASB) are taken from the New American Standard Bible®, © Copyright the Lockman Foundation 1960, 1962, 1963, 1968, 1971, 1972, 1973, 1975, 1995. Used by permission.

All Scripture quotations marked (RSV) are taken from the Revised Standard Version of the Bible, copyright 1952 (RSV) by the Division of Christian Education of the National Council of the Churches of Christ in the USA. All rights reserved. Used by permission.

Pandurang Shastri Athavale. Photo used courtesy of Sat Vichar Darshan Trust.

Vishwa Mohan Bhatt. Photo copyright © Salil V. Bhatt. Used by permission.

J. Carter Brown. Photo copyright © Laura Allen Noel. Used by permission.

David Checketts. Photo copyright © Nat Butler. Used by permission.

Dr. Michael E. DeBakey, M.D. Photo used courtesy of Baylor College of Medicine.

Andre Dubus. Photo copyright © Marion Ettlinger. Used by permission.

Diana Eck. Photo copyright © Lillian Kemp. Used by permission.

Dr. Lorraine Hale. Photo copyright © Shahar Azran. Used by permission.

Benjamin Hirsch. Photo copyright © Jane Leavey. Used by permission.

Ang Lee. Photo copyright © Kenneth S. Lewis. Used by permission.

Madeleine L'Engle. Photo copyright © Kenneth S. Lewis. Used by permission.

Wynton Marsalis. Photo copyright © Frank Stewart. Used by permission.

Kathleen Norris. Photo copyright © David Dwyer. Used by permission.

Hakeem Olajuwon. Photo copyright © Barry Gossage/NBA Photos. Used by permission.

Leontyne Price. Photo copyright © Jack Mitchell. Used by permission.

Rabbi Alexander M. Schindler. Photo copyright © George Kalinsky. Used by permission.

Archbishop Desmond Tutu. Photo used courtesy of the Truth and Reconciliation Commission of South Africa.

Doc Watson. Photo copyright © Kenneth S. Lewis. Used by permission.

Dr. Lori Wiener. Photo copyright © Bill Lebovich. Used by permission.

CONTRIBUTORS

PANDURANG SHASTRI ATHAVALE, a philosopher, was born in 1920 in Roha, India, a small village near Bombay. His father and grandfather were Vedic scholars who taught the young Athavale extensively in studies of Eastern and Western philosophy, comparative religions, literature, grammar, physics, and several languages. Since 1954, he has spearheaded a silent revolution throughout India that aims at the social and cultural transformation of man. Though no formal organization exists, Athavale and his followers have succeeded in creating an enormous "working family" known as *swadhyaya*. The United Nations has named the *swadhyaya* movement one of the most significant developments in the world. In 1997, Athavale was awarded the Templeton Prize for Progress in Religion, which has been given annually since 1973 to a living individual who has shown extraordinary originality in advancing the world's understanding of God and/or spirituality.

HELEN BAYLOR, a gospel recording artist, has released a total of five projects, on compact disc and cassette, on the Word label. These include *Highly Recommended, Look a Little Closer, Start All Over, The Live Experience,* and *Love Brought Me Back.* She has received two Dove awards, three Stellars, one Soultrain Lady of Soul award, and four Grammy nominations. In 1993, she was ordained by her pastor, Dr. Frederick K.C. Price, at her home church, Crenshaw Christian Center, in Riverside, California. In 1995, she received an honorary doctorate degree in Sacred Music from Friends International Christian University, Merced, California. She is the wife of James Baylor and the mother of four children.

HERBERT BENSON, M.D. is the Mind/Body Medical Institute associate professor of medicine, Harvard Medical School; chief of the Division of Behavioral Medicine at the Beth Israel Deaconess Medical Center; and the founding president of the Mind/Body Medical Institute. A graduate of Wesleyan University and the Harvard Medical School, he is the author or co-author of over 150 scientific publications and six books: *The Relaxation Response* (1975), *The Mind/Body Effect* (1979), *Beyond the Relaxation Response* (1984), *Your Maximum Mind* (1987), *The Wellness Book* (1992), *Timeless Healing: The Power and Biology of Belief* (1996). More than four million copies of Dr. Benson's books have been printed. The recipient of numerous national and international awards, he lectures widely and delivers scores of presentations yearly, appearing frequently on national television. His work serves as a bridge between medicine and religion, East and West, mind and body, as well as between belief and science.

VISHWA MOHAN BHATT was born in the Rajput city of Jaipur, India. He has gained international recognition for his performances of Indian classical music on a nineteen-string instrument of revolutionary design and shape, which he invented, called the *mohan veena.* This instrument bears some resemblance to a Western Hawaiian guitar, though Vishwa's style is an assimilation of techniques used on traditional Indian instruments such as the sitar, sarod, and veena.

In addition to his recordings of Indian classical music, Vishwa Mohan Bhatt has been involved in a series of what he refers to as "contemporary fusion projects," in which he has recorded with musicians from other world cultures. His recording *A Meeting by the River,* with American musician Ry Cooder, received a 1994 Grammy award. Other collaborations include *Tabula Rasa,* which features Vishwa with the Chinese erhu player Jei Bing Chen; *Saltanah,* with the Arabian oudh player Simon Shaheen; *Bourbon & Rosewater,* with the American Dobro guitar player Jerry Douglas; and *Mumtaz Mahal,* with the country-blues singer Taj Mahal. According to India's *Hindustan Times,* Vishwa is currently the most popular Indian artist abroad.

J. CARTER BROWN is best known for his accomplishments as director of the National Gallery of Art in Washington, DC, a position he held from 1969 to 1992. During his tenure, Mr. Brown oversaw the transformation of the National Gallery into a multifaceted center for scholarship and public education, with a national and international influence. In 1992, Mr. Brown stepped aside from executive responsibilities of the National Gallery of Art, becoming director emeritus. In addition, he remains the presidentially appointed chairman of the Commission of Fine Arts; chairman of the Leadership Council of the National Cultural Alliance; a trustee of the Kennedy Center; and cofounder and chairman of Ovation, Inc., the Fine Arts Network, a cable television channel devoted exclusively to the arts.

Born in Providence, Rhode Island, Mr. Brown earned an MBA from Harvard University in 1958, and an MA from the Institute of Fine Arts, New York University, in 1961. He has been the recipient of numerous awards, including thirteen honorary degrees and a dozen decorations from foreign nations and the U.S.

GARY CARTER played professional baseball from 1974 to 1992. Throughout his career as a ballplayer, Gary received numerous awards and honors, including his being selected to the National League All-Star Team eleven times. After retiring from baseball in 1992, Gary has worked as a television color commentator for baseball's Florida Marlins (1993 to 1996), and is currently a television color commentator for the Montreal Expos. He has always been active in charity work, and was named sports chairman of the Leukemia Society of America in 1985. Since 1993, Gary has been the president of Baseball Chapel, an organization that provides religious ministry to ballplayers and their families.

DAVID CHECKETTS is president and chief executive officer of Madison Square Garden in New York City. He oversees all operations of the

Garden and its two sports franchises—basketball's Knickerbockers and hockey's Rangers—along with the MSG Television Network, and Radio City Music Hall. In 1983, at age twenty-seven, Dave began a six-year tenure with basketball's Utah Jazz. In 1984, he was promoted to president of the Jazz, becoming the youngest chief executive in the NBA. In addition to his current duties at Madison Square Garden, Dave is involved in many charitable and civic causes.

Monica Geschwind Chusid is president of her own Connecticut-based management consulting firm. Previously in her career she has held management positions at Arthur Andersen & Co. and Ernst & Young. She and her husband, Adam, and her two young daughters, Hannah and Jenna, reside in Westport, Connecticut. When she is not consulting, Monica is writing a book on child care and is actively involved in social action work through her synagogue.

Paulo Coelho is one of Latin America's most beloved writers. His books, including *The Alchemist, The Pilgrimage, By the River Piedra I Sat Down and Wept, The Fifth Mountain,* and *The Valkyries,* have won numerous awards and have become bestsellers in Brazil and around the world. He lives in Rio de Janeiro with his wife, Christine.

Dr. Rama Coomaraswamy was born in New York City in 1929. He entered Harvard University in 1948, and traveled to India in 1951, where he studied Indian history, religion, and culture at Calcutta University. While in Calcutta, Coomaraswamy met Mother Teresa, who was in the beginning stages of her internationally renowned missionary work. Rama became Mother Teresa's first volunteer, and helped her attend to Calcutta's sick and needy. At the encouragement of Mother Teresa, Rama returned to the United States to attend medical school. He graduated from New York University College of Medicine in 1959, and he received board certifications in general surgery (1966), thoracic and cardiovascular surgery (1968), and psychiatry (1996). Dr. Coomaraswamy has published numerous articles and essays in the fields of surgery, philosophy, and comparative religion. His father, the late

Ananda K. Coomaraswamy, was internationally renowned as a philosopher, writer, and Orientalist, and was curator of Indian art at the Boston Museum of Fine Arts.

MICHAEL E. DEBAKEY, M.D. is internationally recognized as an ingenious medical inventor and innovator, a gifted and dedicated teacher, a premier surgeon, and an international medical statesman. Dr. DeBakey served as chancellor of Baylor College of Medicine from 1979 to 1996, as president from 1969 to 1979, and as chairman of the Department of Surgery from 1948 to 1993. He now serves as the chancellor emeritus, distinguished service professor, and Olga Keith Weiss Professor of Surgery, and director of the DeBakey Heart Center, which was established by Baylor in 1985 for research and public education in the prevention and treatment of heart disease. He has served as advisor to almost every U.S. president in the past fifty years and to heads of state throughout the world.

Dr. DeBakey's impressive, lifelong scholarship is reflected in more than fourteen hundred medical articles, chapters, and books he has published on various aspects of surgery, medicine, health, medical research, and medical education—many of these are now considered classics. In addition to his scholarly writings, he is co-author of several bestselling books for the general public, including *The Living Heart* (1977), *The Living Heart Diet* (1984), *The Living Heart Brand Name Shopper's Guide* (1993), and *The New Living Heart Diet* (1996).

ALAN M. DERSHOWITZ is a noted lawyer and leading defender of individual rights. He is the author of the bestsellers *Chutzpah, Reversal of Fortune, Reasonable Doubts: The Criminal Justice System and the O. J. Simpson Case,* and *The Best Defense,* as well as *The Vanishing American Jew, The Abuse Excuse,* and *The Advocate's Devil.* At twenty-eight years old, he became the youngest full professor appointed to the Harvard law faculty. He is also a newspaper columnist, and a frequent guest on television and radio programs. He lectures widely on Jewish issues, such as anti-Semitism, cultural identity, the Holocaust, assimilation, and Israeli-U.S. relations.

MARK DOTY is the author of four books of poetry, including *My Alexandria* (1993), which was chosen for the National Poetry Series by Philip Levine and won the National Book Critics Circle Award, Britain's T.S. Eliot Prize, the Los Angeles Times Book Prize, and was a finalist for the National Book Award. *Atlantis* (1995) was named a Notable Book of the Year by both *The New York Times* and the American Library Association, and received the Bingham Poetry Prize, the Ambassador Book Award, and a Lambda Literary Award. A new collection of poems, *Sweet Machine,* is forthcoming from HarperCollins in 1998. His memoir, *Heaven's Coast* (1996), won the PEN Martha Albrand Award for Nonfiction, and was named a Notable Book of the Year by *The New York Times Book Review.*

ANDRE DUBUS is the author of nine books of fiction, including *Dancing After Hours* (1996), *Selected Stories* (1989), *The Last Worthless Evening* (1986), *Voices from the Moon* (1984), *Finding a Girl in America* (1979), and *Separate Flights* (1975), as well as two collection of essays, *Meditations from a Moveable Chair* (1998) and *Broken Vessels* (1991). He has received the PEN/Malamud Award, the Jean Stein Award from the American Academy of Arts and Letters, the *Boston Globe*'s first annual Lawrence L. Winship Award, and fellowships from both the Guggenheim and MacArthur foundations. He has been a Marine Corps captain, a college teacher, and a member of the Iowa Writers' Workshop.

DIANA ECK is Professor of Comparative Religion and Indian Studies at Harvard University, where she is also chair of the Committee on the Study of Religion in the Faculty of Arts and Sciences. She is also a member of the Department of Sanskrit and Indian Studies as well as the Faculty of Divinity. Her most recent book, *Encountering God: A Spiritual Journey from Bozeman to Banaras* (1993), is in the area of Christian theology and interfaith dialogue. Since 1991, she has been heading a research team at Harvard University to explore the new religious diversity of the United States and its meaning for the American pluralist experiment. The Pluralism Project has been documenting the growing presence of the Muslim, Buddhist, Hindu, Sikh, Jain, and Zoroastrian communities in the U.S. In 1997, the Pluralism Project's interactive CD-ROM, *On Common Ground: World Religions in America,* a multimedia introduction to the world's religions in the American context, was published by Columbia University Press.

HOWARD FINSTER, born in 1916 in Valley Head, Alabama, is a renowned and respected folk artist, who has had art showings around the world, including the Library of Congress and the Smithsonian Institute. He has taught students in college workshops across the U.S., and has been featured in many magazines, newspapers, and television broadcasts. He is the creator of Paradise Gardens, located in his hometown of Summerville, Georgia. Paradise Gardens is a maze of sculptures and structures, with the pervasive presence of Scriptures, their lessons, and Howard's "messages" from God. Thousands of visitors come to Paradise Gardens each year, making it one of Georgia's top-ten tourist attractions. Howard frequently greets visitors on Sundays from 2:00 P.M. till 5:00 P.M.

DR. LORRAINE HALE holds doctoral degrees in child development and developmental psychology, and is co-founder and president of Hale House, a home for children who are born addicted to drugs and alcohol, and whose mothers cannot care for them. Hale House, founded in 1969 by Dr. Hale and her mother, the late Clara Hale, was the first nonprofit child care agency in the United States established exclusively for children of drug-addicted mothers. It rose to international attention in 1986 when President Ronald Reagan appointed both Clara and Lorraine Hale to his National Drug Free America Task Force. The Hales' efforts to bring help and hope to the desperate needs of inner-city lives have resulted in the development of several other programs, including the Community-Based Family program, which offers peer support and adult mentors for troubled youngsters; the founding of a home for mothers and their babies who are suffering from AIDS; and the Homeward Bound program, which helps mothers who are recovering from drug addiction re-enter society and assume their parental responsibilities.

KARI LEE HART was born in 1956 in Cambridge, Massachusetts. She graduated from Oberlin College in 1978 with a degree in American history. She has worked as a copy editor, fitness instructor, and day-care provider and has held many positions in various community organizations. She is currently enrolled at the Lutheran Theological Seminary in Philadelphia, Pennsylvania, where she is pursuing a Master of Divinity degree. She resides in Philadelphia with her husband, Shawn, and her two daughters, Katie and Amanda.

BENJAMIN HIRSCH was born in Frankfurt am Main, Germany, in 1932. He eluded the Nazi forces with the help of the French Jewish network, and escaped to the United States in 1941. He served in the U.S. army from 1953 to 1955, graduated from the Georgia Institute of Technology's School of Architecture in 1958, and is a practicing architect, whose firm designs commercial, industrial, institutional, and residential projects locally while specializing, on a national level, in the design of synagogues and churches. He has received three National Design Awards in the field of religious architecture. He is the design architect, concept developer, and exhibit designer for the *Absence of Humanity: The Holocaust Years* exhibition in Atlanta's William Breman Jewish Heritage Museum. As a guest lecturer, Benjamin Hirsch speaks to many school and adult groups as a personal witness to, and student of, the Holocaust.

SIMON JACOBSON is a member of the Lubavitch movement of Chassidus, and resides in the Crown Heights section of Brooklyn, New York. He is the author of the bestseller *Toward a Meaningful Life: The Wisdom of the Rebbe,* in which he presents, for the first time in English, the teachings of the legendary Lubavitcher leader Rabbi Menachem Mendel Schneerson. Currently, he is editor in chief of *Vaad Hanochos Hatmimim,* a foundation dedicated to preserving and perpetuating Rabbi Schneerson's teachings. Rabbi Jacobson also teaches a class on spirituality every Wednesday evening on the Upper West Side of New York City.

ANG LEE was born in Taiwan in 1954 and moved to the U.S. in 1978, where he received his BFA in theater from the University of Illinois, and his MFA in film production from New York University. *Pushing Hands* (1992), his debut as a feature film director, won numerous awards and garnered much critical praise. In addition to *Pushing Hands,* Ang has directed *The Wedding Banquet* (1993), *Eat Drink Man Woman* (1994), *Sense and Sensibility* (1995), and *The Ice Storm* (1996).

MADELEINE L'ENGLE is the internationally known, award-winning author of more than forty books for readers of all ages, including *A Wrinkle in Time,* which was a 1963 Newbery Medal winner; *Two-Part Invention; A Swiftly Tilting Planet,* which received the American Book Award; *The Irrational Season; A Wind in the Door; The Glorious Impossible;* and *A Ring of Endless Light,* which was a 1981 Newbery Honor Book. Madeleine frequently lectures at writers' conferences, leads retreats, and addresses church and student groups. She has interspersed her prolific writing career with raising three children and maintaining an apartment in New York City and a Connecticut farmhouse called "Crosswicks."

WALTER LEVINE has been successful in many business ventures, including investment banking, real estate, home security alarm systems, video and audio production, and entertainment management. In 1990, Walter was diagnosed with multiple myeloma cancer and given a prognosis of having only three days to live. Rather than giving up, through self-determination, the support and love of his family and friends, and through prayer, Walter fought the cancer and won. Since his recovery from cancer, Walter has dedicated himself to helping others beat this disease. He and his wife, Fritzie, have four children and seven grandchildren.

WYNTON MARSALIS, born in 1961, is the most accomplished and acclaimed jazz musician and composer of his generation. He is also one of the world's leading classical trumpet virtuosos. Winner of numerous Grammy awards, he made history in 1983 as the first artist to win Grammys in both the jazz and classical fields, an achievement he went on to repeat the following year. Among his many other awards, he has received the Grand Prix du Disque of France, the Edison Award of the Netherlands, and was elected an honorary member of England's Royal Academy of Music. He is artistic director of the internationally recognized Jazz at Lincoln Center program, which he co-founded in 1987. Several commissioned works for the program are among his most recent successes as a composer, including *Blood on the Fields,* his epic oratorio on slavery, which won the 1997 Pulitzer prize for music. This was the first Pulitzer ever awarded in the field of jazz. Throughout his career, Wynton has devoted considerable time to music education for children and students. He won a Peabody Award in 1996 for his informative twenty-six-part National Public Radio series, *Making the Music,* and his four-part PBS series, *Marsalis on Music.*

RICK MOODY is the author of the novels *Garden State* (1992), which won the Pushcart Editor's Choice Award, *The Ice Storm* (1994), and *Purple America* (1997). The title piece from his story collection *The Ring of Brightest Angels Around Heaven* (1995) won the *Paris Review*'s Aga Khan Prize. He is co-editor with Darcey Steinke of an anthology, *Joyful Noise: The New Testament Revisited* (1998). Rick has contributed stories and essays to many publications, including *The New Yorker, Esquire, Harpers, The Paris Review, Grand Street,* and *The New York Times.* He lives in Brooklyn, New York.

THOMAS MOORE is the author of several bestselling books, including *Care of the Soul* (1992), *Soul Mates* (1994), *Meditations: On the Monk Who Dwells in Daily Life* (1994), *The Education of the Heart* (1996), and *The Re-Enchantment of Everyday Life* (1996). He is the author, or subject, of numerous audio and video productions; is a former professor of religion and psychology; and has degrees in theology, musicology, and philosophy. He was a monk in a Catholic seminary for twelve years, and currently lives in New Hampshire with his wife and two children.

KATHLEEN NORRIS is an award-winning poet and the author of *The Cloister Walk* (1996), which was a *New York Times* bestseller and Notable Book of the Year, *Dakota: A Spiritual Geography* (1993), *Amazing Grace: A Vocabulary of Faith* (1998), *The Quotidian Mysteries: Laundry, Liturgy, and Women's Work* (1998), and three volumes of poetry, including *Little Girls in Church* (1995). Her poetry and essays have appeared in numerous magazines and anthologies. A recipient of grants from the Bush and Guggenheim foundations, she has been in residence twice at the Institute for Ecumenical and Cultural Research at St. John's Abbey in Collegeville, Minnesota. For over ten years, she has been an oblate of Assumption Abbey in North Dakota.

HAKEEM OLAJUWON is consistently among the National Basketball Association's leaders in scoring, rebounding, blocked shots, and steals. As the first selection in the 1984 NBA draft, Hakeem transformed the Houston Rockets' worst-ever team (14–68 in 1982–83) into Western Conference champions and an NBA finalist in just his second season. He led the Rockets to back-to-back NBA championships (1993–94, 1994–95) and was a member of the U.S. Olympic Dream Team, which won the gold medal in 1996. In 1994, Hakeem created his Dream Foundation to encourage education as a way of realizing one's dreams. The foundation provides college scholarship funds for Houston-area students.

CHRISTOPHER PARKENING is one of the world's preeminent virtuosos of the classical guitar. For over twenty-five years, his recordings and concert performances have been greeted with the highest acclaim. He has appeared on many nationally broadcast television programs and specials, and has been a frequent guest soloist with the world's finest orchestras. He has also authored two instructional books, *The Christopher Parkening Guitar Method, Volumes 1 and 2.* In addition to his excellence in music, Christopher is a world-class fly-fishing and casting champion. Since 1982, Christopher has proclaimed a deep and significant commitment to the Christian faith.

KATHERINE PATERSON was born in 1932 in Qing Jiang, Jiangsu, China, the daughter of Presbyterian missionaries, and came to the United States at the age of eight. Her books have been published in twenty-two languages and have won awards in the United States and abroad. She has twice been awarded the National Book Award for children's literature and the Newbery Award. Her books have also garnered a Newbery Honor Award, Christopher Medal, and Scott O'Dell Award for historical fiction, Le Grand Prix des Jeunes Lecteurs, France and the Janusz Korczak Medal, Poland.

Katherine Paterson's many books include *The Sign of the Chrysanthemum* (1973), *Bridge to Terabithia* (1977), *The Great Gilly Hopkins* (1978), *Jacob Have I Loved* (1980), *Come Sing, Jimmy Jo* (1985), *Lyddie* (1991), and *Flip-Flop Girl* (1994). She is also the author of the excellent *A Sense of Wonder* (1995), a collection of essays on reading and writing for children. For the body of her work, she is the recipient of nine honorary doctorates, and other honors, including the Regina Medal, and is for the third time the U.S. nominee for the international Hans Christian Andersen Medal.

JACK POLAK was born in 1912, in Amsterdam, the Netherlands. He studied tax law and became a certified tax consultant in 1937. In 1943, during the Nazi occupation of the Netherlands, his parents were deported to Sobibor, where they died in the gas chambers. He was taken to the Dutch deportation camp Westerbork, and was later sent to the concentration camp Bergen-Belsen. He was liberated by the Russian army on April 23, 1945. In 1946, Jack Polak married Catharina, whom he had met and "courted" in the camps. The couple had two children, and emigrated to the United States in 1951. Jack became a professional investment counselor, and has served as director of several public companies.

In 1992, on Jack's eightieth birthday, he was knighted by Queen Beatrix of the Netherlands for his work as the chairman of the Anne Frank Center, USA, and for speaking at universities and organizations on the history of the Jews in the Netherlands. This is comparable with the Medal of Honor in the United States. In 1997, Jack received the

Louis E. Yavner Citizen Award for Outstanding Contributions to Teaching About the Holocaust and Other Violations of Human Rights.

JOHN POLKINGHORNE has had a distinguished career as a particle physicist. He is the author of books that explore themes in science and religion, including *Belief in God in an Age of Science* (1998), *Beyond Science* (1996), *Quarks, Chaos, & Christianity* (1995), *The Faith of a Physicist* (1994), *Reason and Reality* (1991), *Science and Providence* (1989), *Science and Creation* (1988), and *The Way the World Is* (1984). In 1974 he was elected a Fellow of the Royal Society, and was Professor of Mathematical Physics at the University of Cambridge in 1968–79. In 1982 he was ordained as a priest in the Anglican Church. From 1989–96 he was the president of Queens' College, Cambridge.

LEONTYNE PRICE, the internationally renowned opera singer, was born in 1927 in Laurel, Mississippi. Her professional opera debut took place in Paris, in 1952, with a performance of *Four Saints in Three Acts* by Virgil Thompson. In 1955, the NBC Opera Company's production of *Tosca* introduced Leontyne to a nationwide American audience. This performance was noteworthy because it was the first time a black artist had performed in opera on television. Her legendary association with New York's Metropolitan Opera House began in 1961—a year in which she appeared in the major soprano role of six grand operas—and continued until 1985, when at the age of fifty-seven, and after 178 Met performances, she retired from the operatic stage. Leontyne Price continues, to this day, to perform concerts and recitals.

STEVE REICH was born in 1936 in New York. Since the mid-1960s, he has been recognized internationally for his achievements in the field of music composition. The spare and stark qualities of his earliest works often identified him with the Minimalist movement. He has evolved, over the past thirty years, as a composer of complex vision. With compositions including *Music for 18 Musicians, The Desert Music, Electric Counterpoint, The Cave, Tehillim,* and *Proverb,* Steve Reich has continuously redefined contemporary classical music. His 1988 recording, *Dif-*

ferent Trains, which features the Kronos Quartet, was awarded the Grammy award for classical composition.

MARK RICHARD (pronounced in the French manner) was born in 1955 in Lake Charles, Louisiana, and grew up in Texas and Virginia. He is the author of two story collections and a novel. His first collection, *The Ice at the Bottom of the World,* received the PEN/Hemingway Award in 1990. After the third printing of his novel *Fishboy* (1993), he was the subject of a two-part profile in *The New York Times Book Review* on the marketing of a first novel. *Charity,* his second story collection, was published in 1998.

Mark Richard has received the Whiting Foundation Writers' Award and the Hobson Prize, as well as fellowships from the National Endowment for the Arts and the New York Foundation for the Arts. His stories have appeared in *Esquire, The New Yorker, Harpers,* the *Paris Review,* the *Oxford American, Grand Street, Antaeus, Shenandoah,* and *Equator,* and they have been anthologized in such collections as *Best American Short Stories,* the *Pushcart Prize Stories,* and *New Stories from the South.* His journalism has appeared in *Spin, George, Vogue,* and elsewhere, and he is a correspondent for BBC radio.

FAITH RINGGOLD, painter, mixed-media sculptor, performance artist, and writer, was born in Harlem in 1930, and lives and works in La Jolla, California, and Englewood, New Jersey. She is the recipient of more than seventy-five awards, including eleven honorary Doctor of Fine Arts degrees, and many other fellowships and grants. Her art has been exhibited in museums and galleries in the USA, Europe, Asia, South America, the Middle East, and Africa.

Faith Ringgold's first published book, *Tar Beach* (1991), has won more than thirty awards, including the Caldecott Honor and the Coretta Scott King Award for the best-illustrated children's book of 1991. Ringgold has written and illustrated a total of five children's books, including *Tar Beach, Aunt Harriet's Railroad in the Sky, My Dream of Martin Luther King, Dinner at Aunt Connie's House,* and *Bonjour Lonnie.* She has also published *Talking to Faith Ringgold* (an autobiographical interactive art book for children of all ages), and *We Flew Over the Bridge: The Memoirs of Faith Ringgold* (her first adult book).

JEAN-PIERRE RUIZ, a Roman Catholic priest of the diocese of Brooklyn, New York, teaches in the department of theology and religious studies at St. John's University, Jamaica, New York. Father Ruiz is past president (1995–96) of the Academy of Catholic Hispanic Theologians of the United States and editor in chief of the *Journal of Hispanic/ Latino Theology.* The author of one book and numerous articles in academic journals and other periodicals, he is currently working on a commentary on the book of the prophet Ezekiel.

JEFFREY B. SATINOVER, M.D., has had a long association with leaders of both Jewish and Christian spirituality as well as wide-ranging expertise in mathematics and physics, laboratory science, and clinical psychiatry. A practicing psychiatrist and former William James Lecturer at Harvard, he holds degrees from the Massachusetts Institute of Technology, the Harvard Graduate School of Education, and the University of Texas. Currently, he is studying physics at Yale, where he is a former fellow in adult and child psychiatry.

Dr. Satinover lectures widely on topics ranging from brain neurophysiology to the breakdown of modern society. He is on the national board of governors of Toward Tradition, an organization of Protestants, Catholics, and Jews working toward the restoration of traditional moral standards in America. His most recent book, *Cracking the Bible Code,* was published in 1997 by William Morrow.

ALEXANDER M. SCHINDLER is one of the most influential leaders in all of American Judaism. As president from 1973 to 1996 of the Union of American Hebrew Congregations (UAHC), Reform Judaism's main governing body, Rabbi Schindler built the movement into one of the most vigorous forces in American religious life. He became renowned for his unrelenting commitment to issues of peace, social justice, and equality. He presently serves as president of the Memorial

Foundation for Jewish Culture and vice president of the World Jewish Congress.

Born in Germany in 1925, Rabbi Schindler fled the Nazis with his family, arriving in the U.S. when he was twelve. He earned a Purple Heart and Bronze Star for bravery in action as a U.S. army ski-trooper in Europe, and graduated from the College of the City of New York before studying for the rabbinate at Hebrew Union College.

DESMOND TUTU, archbishop of South Africa, is one of the great inspirational leaders of our age. He won the Nobel Peace Prize in 1984, and has been the recipient of many honorary degrees from the world's major institutions of learning. He is well-known throughout the world for his opposition to apartheid, and for his leadership in the struggle for nonviolent liberation in South Africa. He is the author of *An African Prayer Book* and *The Rainbow People of God,* which traces South Africa's victory over apartheid.

DOC WATSON is a legendary performer who blends his traditional Appalachian musical roots with bluegrass, country, gospel, and blues to create a unique style and an expansive repertoire. He is the recipient of numerous awards, including the National Medal of Arts, the National Heritage Fellowship, and five Grammy awards.

Doc was born Arthel L. Watson in Deep Gap, North Carolina, in 1923. His mother, Annie Watson, sang traditional secular and religious songs, and his father, General Watson, played banjo and was church singing leader. Through the influence of his parents, and through his musical studies at the Raleigh School for the Blind, Doc emerged as a powerful singer and a tremendously influential picker who virtually invented the art of playing mountain fiddle tunes on the flattop guitar. It wasn't until 1953, at age thirty, that Doc began to play musical dates for pay. By the early sixties, he was a full-time professional, playing a wide range of concerts, clubs, colleges, and festivals, including the Newport Folk Festival and Carnegie Hall. In the seventies, Doc toured with his son, Merle, who provided musical and emotional companionship. In 1985, Merle died in a tractor accident, and Doc stopped performing for a brief period of time. He now accepts a limited number of engagements per year.

DR. LORI WIENER is the coordinator of the Pediatric HIV Psychosocial Support Program at the National Cancer Institute, located in Bethesda, Maryland. She was hired by the institute in 1986 to help the chief of the pediatric branch incorporate HIV disease into the existing pediatric oncology program. Dr. Wiener has been working in the field of HIV/AIDS since 1982. She is co-author of *Be a Friend: Children Who Live with HIV Speak* (1994).

TOBIAS WOLFF is the award-winning author of the memoirs *This Boy's Life* (1989) and *In Pharaoh's Army* (1994). He is also regarded as being a master of the short story, and his short fiction is available in the collections *In the Garden of the North American Martyrs* (1981), *Back in the World* (1985), and *The Night in Question* (1996). His short novel, *The Barracks Thief,* won the 1985 PEN/Faulkner Award. He lives with his family in upstate New York, and teaches at Syracuse University.

INDEX

Kittredge, Mary, on breath of God in
myths, 19
Kosher dietary laws, 171

Lectio, 182
Lee, Ang
on Buddhism, 109
communal ceremony prior to
filming, 188–90
on creativity, 107–8, 110
L'Engle, Madeleine
on discipline of creativity, 9, 118–19
on divine inspiration, 29–30
on prayer, 138
Levine, Walter, cancer survivor, 66–69
Lewis, C. S., 27
Light, as symbol, 174
Listening, 9, 107, 137, 146
See also Meditation
Liszt, Franz, 125
Liturgy of the Hours, 128, 145
Lord's Prayer, 165–67
Loss
Dubus on, 42–45
Moore on, 148
See also Death
Love
God's, for man, 26, 37, 53–54, 57,
194–95
inspiration and, 8, 28, 45
Saint Paul on, 125

MacArthur, John, 86
Magnificent Defeat, The (Buechner),
93–94, 133–34
Maimonides Prayer, 151
Marsalis, Wynton
on divine inspiration, 122–23
on prayer, 161
Materialism, unfulfilling nature of, 85–
86, 87–88, 91
Mathematics, 98, 99

Meditation
achieving focus/perspective through,
136, 137
Buddhist practice of, 107
focus on breath in, 37–38, 137
ritual and, 171
without religious foundation, 64, 172
See also Prayer
Mental illness, faith conquering, 59–60
Merton, Thomas, 111, 144–45
Metaphor, in films, 110
Miracles, 23, 51
Mitzvoth, 33, 34, 171
Monastic life, Kathleen Norris on, 128,
181–82
Moody, Rick
background, 58
on communal worship, 189–90
faith conquers depression, 59–60
on humility, 61, 62
on prayer, 138–39
Moore, Thomas, 146–48
Mother Teresa, 66, 68–69
Music
Hindu devotional, 115
Marsalis on, 122–23
Parkening on, 86–87
Reich on, 124
as theology, 15, 87
Watson on, 25
See also Creativity; Singing
Muslims. *See* Islam
My Dream of Martin Luther King
(Ringgold), 120, 121
Mystery, 23, 51, 141, 148
of creativity, 96, 106, 112, 113, 126
See also Science and religion
Myths, breath of God image in, 19

Near-death experiences, 55
New Testament, 50, 152
See also Scripture
Nonbelievers, 109
healing and, 28, 48, 62, 151
inspiration and, 10, 111
prayer and, 133–34